Fruit of the Spirit

I Thank you and Appreciate your Support, may GOD Continue to Bless and Keep you In perfect peace..

Fruit of the Spirit

The World's Greatest Poet

Darryl Cannady

Giving honor to my LORD and Savior
JESUS CHRIST . . .

Library of Congress Control Number:		2013907722
ISBN:	Hardcover	978-1-4836-3338-1
	Softcover	978-1-4836-3337-4
	Ebook	978-1-4836-3339-8

This book was printed in the United States of America.

Rev. date: 06/08/2013

To order additional copies of this book, contact:
Xlibris Corporation
1-888-795-4274
www.Xlibris.com
Orders@Xlibris.com
131478

Contents

Dedication

TO MY MOTHER, GLORIA CANNADY, I LOVE YOU

MY WIFE, BELINDA CANNADY THANKS FOR ENDURING THE TEDIOUS PROCESS OF WRITING AND PUBLISHING.

MY KIDS, DE'MANTE, MICHAEL, JA'LICIA, DARRELL, YASMIN, LIZZIE, CHASITY

IN MEMORY OF MY SISTER

SHEILA (REDD) CANNADY

SPECIAL THANKS TO: MAYA ANGELOU FOR YOUR INSPIRATION AND LEADERSHIP.

SPECIAL THANKS TO: BISHOP ALONZO RODGERS FOR YOUR GUIDANCE AND GREAT LEADERSHIP YOU HAVE BLESSED MY LIFE IN WAYS YOU WILL NEVER KNOW.

SPECIAL THANKS TO: MY PASTOR MY FRIEND AND EDUCATOR ELDER VERLON J. POMPEY FOR BELIEVING AND HAVING FAITH IN ME.

SPECIAL THANKS TO: REV.JOSEPH A. SUTTON MY MENTOR

FOR NOT ONLY BELIEVING IN ME AND ENCOURAGING ME BUT ALSO FOR YOUR GUIDANCE AND FRIENDSHIP.

THANK YOU ALL FOR YOUR PRAYERS.

Introduction

Some poems in this book will make you laugh
some poems may make you cry,
these poems you read are inspired by GOD
wipe dry your teary eyes,
the poems you read are not about me
but about my Savior CHRIST,
to help some to overcome despair
and lead some to eternal life . . .

Yesterday

GOD can take a cloud
and let the sun shine through,
GOD can take the grass and weeds
and saturate them with His dew,
GOD can take trouble
and move it's mountain out of the way,
GOD can cast out demons
and heal the sick like yesterday.
GOD can give us love
to cover a multitude of sin,
GOD can make the blind to see
the lame to walk again,
GOD can take 2 fish
and feed 5000 by His array,
GOD can raise the dead
like He did yesterday
GOD can teach the sheep
sometime they still will go astray,
GOD can give you power to overcome what's in your way,
although we are undeserving He shows us love always
GOD wants none of us to perish
like He did yesterday . . .

Just A Tool

What good am I if a person is down
and I can't help them stand,
it's not my job to hold them there
if I can't lend a hand,
when someone is going through something
and trials in life seem hard,
I just want to make a difference
by being a tool in the hand of the Lord,
When people need a shoulder
they can lean on me,
I want to be a light unto their darkened path
so bright that they can see,
I don't agree with what some people do
it's not my job to tear them apart,
I just want to make a difference
by being a tool in the hand of the Lord,
Though if you pray to GOD for a garden
pray with a hoe in your hand,
He will bless you more for meeting Him halfway
than always coming with just your plan,
but if I see you laboring and I'm nearby
I will be glad to do my part,
for I just want to make a difference
by being a tool in the hand of the Lord.

Upmost Gratitude

There are no words to express
how grateful that I am,
or no scale that I could weigh
my gratitude by the gram,
when I thought no one was there
to carry my problems to,
You were there to lend a hand
You came quickly to my rescue,
today I want to say
a few words that ring so true,
thanks for all You've done for me
You have my utmost gratitude.
There is a friend that sticks closer than a brother
that one is JESUS CHRIST,
and in this world He crossed our paths
knowing You would change my life,
I do not come with eloquent speech
but I come straight from my heart,
I thank GOD for You being in my life and playing such special part,
so today I want to say a few words that ring so true
thanks for all You've done for me,
You have my utmost gratitude . . .

The Tie That Binds

Blest be the tie that binds
JESUS CHRIST life to mine,
GOD the merciful creator of time
magnificent the most divine,
there is no other source to go
who pours His grace on us below,
the word that comes to us from old
the most wonderful story ever told,
the tie that binds keeps me from falling
to the depths of hell below,
allows me the HOLY SPIRIT
and life's lessons to help me grow,
the tie that binds and grips my hands
let's nothing rip me apart,
is GOD almighty who sent His son
just to win my heart . . .

God Is Always There

I have been to the bottom of the valley
fell off the mountain peak,
so low I've touched despair
so low I couldn't be reached,
thought GOD had turned His back on me
and rejected my every prayer,
lo' and behold it was He who guided my feet
GOD was always there,
I have scraped the bottom of the sea
could not swim even with fins
Felt like a ton of bricks tied around my neck
I was weighed down by many sin,
it was at my lowest ebb
before I became aware,
there was a power bigger than myself
who had love for me and cared,
so I looked towards His abode
and lifted up my prayers,
lo' and behold it is He who guides my feet
GOD is always there . . .

Be Patient

It's hard to be patient and wait
when you want something to happen right now,
but pray to GOD in faith
and He will work it out,
when no solution seems is near,
and your problem has been prolonged,
GOD hasn't turned His back on you
patience just makes you strong,
His time is not our time
we must keep this in mind,
I've never seen the righteous forsaken
nor His seed begging and bound,
when things sometime seem worst
you're biting your nails to impatient to wait
GOD will give you endurance,
to make it through just one more day . . . .

Martyr In Meekness

I want to be a martyr for CHRIST
what greater privilege than to be persecuted
for Him in this life,
martyrs are meek but they are never weak
meekness implies a teachable spirit,
the world thinks in terms of strength and power
self-assurance and possession,
a Christian should worry about His soul
and constant progression,
(Matthew 11:29) "Take my yoke upon you and learn of me;
for I am meek and lowly in heart:
and you shall find rest unto your souls."
We need to crucify our old self
along with CHRIST and let GOD have total control.
When things rise up against us
and appears unfair
there is one door always open
who hears our every prayer

I Surrender

GOD, I surrender
give up my will
now let your will be done,
for I have failed
in all I've tried
now I shall try your son.
I surrender! I surrender!
Didn't know life could be so hard
I have tried most everything
now I shall try the LORD . . .

How Deep Is His Love

The love of GOD is deep and great
deeper than man's deepest hate
deeper than any heart could sink
or any words a brain could think
deeper than any amount of dirt
deeper than any feelings hurt
deeper than any wrong that's done
so deep He sent His only son
money could never repay the cost
that saves a soul from being lost. That deep . . . .

Clouds And Rain

Just sit still and GOD will speak
reveal Himself to you,
tear down the strongholds of your heart
and build your life anew,
definitely renew your strength
just humble yourself real low,
then GOD will move within your heart
and help your life to grow,
best place for Him to do His work
is prison or in jail,
where He can deal with one
one on one
while sitting in a cell,
sometimes He has to chastise us
allowing us to be contained,
when we are hard headed
and will not listen
storms bring clouds and rain . . .

Hmmm

Could a policeman sit by eating
and worried about himself,
while a person is in distress
and needs someone quick to help? Hmmm . . .
Could a lifeguard sit by watching
while a drowning person dies?
Could a mother know her baby is hungry
but instead just let him cry? Hmmm . . .
Can GOD make us promises
then flat out tell a lie?(not)
How can we say that we are Christians
and yet our actions deny? Hmmm . . .

Good Anchor

Will your anchor hold firm
through the storms of life
so your vessel doesn't blow away,
will it hold when hurricanes come
and let you stay through another day,
will it remain when the waves beat upon it
with noise the sound of thunder,
will your anchor hold the vessel firm
or let your ship go under,
will it ground and hold the boat
or in vain just let it float,
or fasten onto solid rock
strengthened by JESUS' rope,
will it hold when whirlpools try
to turn you 'round and 'round,
will your anchor hold your vessel firm
or let your ship go down . . .

The Heart . . .

The face is a mirror of the heart
do people see CHRIST in you,
can they tell by the way you
walk and in everything you do?
Does your heart radiate love
and touch someone's life in depth,
is your heart cold or warm
is your heart one eager to help,
is your heart forever kind
to that one hard to love,
is your heart wise as a serpent
is it humble as a dove,
the face is a mirror of the heart
do people see CHRIST in you,
can they tell by the way you walk
and in everything you do?

Can You Stand the Storm

When the sun is shining in your life
there's no reason for alarm,
everybody loves the calm
but can you stand the storm,
does your spirit dwindle low
when clouds bring drenching rain,
or will your heart remain the same
in the midst of a hurricane,
GOD is searching for a soldier
who will fight throughout the war,
and will stand though his faith's been tried
and his spirit has been scarred,
but his hope is in the LORD
who makes opposition surrender,
the one who claims the victory
in CHRIST becomes the winner,
when the Son is shining in your life
and no reason for alarm,
everybody loves the calm
but can you stand the storm . . .

Witness

As I look back at the rugged road
and see how far I've traveled,
while I was in sinking sand
GOD placed my feet on gravel,
He strengthened me when I was weak
gave peace to all my trouble,
He sent His only begotten Son
that all my sin be covered,
His miracles are still working today
I am a witness what GOD can do,
all the problems in this life I've faced
my GOD has brought me through,
He was with Shadrach, Meshach and Abednego
when they were in the fire,
He was with Daniel in the lion's den
my GOD He never tires,
He was with Joseph throughout His ordeal
and David when He slew the giant,
so I know He will be with me
because in Him is my reliance,
His miracles still are working today
I am a miracle of what He can do,
all the problems in this life that I have faced
my GOD has brought me through . . .

Green Leaved Valley

How deep the green leaved valley
now unveiled with distant haze,
GOD is way beyond magnificent
and I humbly give Him praise,
love blows gently across the hills
like ne'er before clouds at dawn,
grace and mercy in the air
destination is unknown,
how deep is the heart
to seek and find true joy within,
knows the source from which it comes
invites an ever present friend,
how deep the green leaved valley
now veiled with distant haze,
GOD is way beyond magnificent
and I humbly give Him praise . . .

Always On Time

The storm has come and gone
it left a strengthened spirit,
GOD removed it just in time
for my soul was getting weary,
my patience had been tried
and barely did pass the test,
thought often of giving up
for my mind needed rest,
the point I felt I could take no more
a blessing came no room to store,
"oh ye of little faith" GOD spoke clearly in my ear,
"how many times have I delivered you
when your trouble was so near"
Now I exercise my faith
I leave my problems up to Him,
He always comes right on time
when life sometime seem dim . . .

The Trickster

The best magician in this world is satan
he is the master of his kind,
he gives illusions that cause confusion
the most elect he will blind,
he'll leave you awed and astounded
amazed and hallucinating,
he will leave you dumb and profound
these are the tricks of satan,
everything he says is a lie
doesn't want the truth to prevail,
he will trick the most intellectual out of his mind
and lead his soul straight to hell . . .

Writhing Storms

I've fought death and won the battle
with no strength though of my own,
writhing storms have over whelmed me
through them all GOD made me strong,
I was raised a decent person
my mother never spared the rod,
carried me to church most every Sunday
instilled in me the fear of GOD,
though I only had my dreams
thought I'd never leave the ghetto,
GOD gave me His favor
writhing storms I've had to weather,
been attacked by satan often
benefits sometimes come hard,
I've had numerous fights with patience
but stayed focused on GOD'S reward,
nothing will dissuade me
I can't be plucked out JESUS' hand,
writhing storms sometime drench me
though I waver still I stand . . .

He Cares

As I live day by day sometimes it feels like I'm alone,
the ones that GOD have blessed me with
are busy sometimes gone,
so I look for comfort in JESUS
who lets me know that He is there,
and I confide within His arms cause I know my Savior cares
when you can't depend on family
place your faith in the LORD,
He will help you when in need
there's no problem to Him thats hard,
doesn't matter what plight or peril He is able to subdue,
and control the storms within your life He will bring you through,
so I look for comfort in JESUS who lets me know that He is there,
and I confide within His arms because I know my Savior cares . . .

Profound

In the evening eastern sky
as I watch the sun to set,
I've lived and breathed another day
without a single regret,
GOD'S beauty is profound
no words describe it's scene,
serenity entices the eye to see
it's contrast is so keen,
takes the mind off reality it's similar to a dream,
His colors are so beautiful like coffee mixed with cream,
His grace is so sufficient
His holiness is supreme,
I keep my heart within His hand
oh, all the joy He brings,
and when I feel so burdened
and my joy has withered down,
I look towards heaven and rejoice
for His grace is so profound . . .

Praise Him

"Like a sheep before the shearer
(Isaiah 53:7) He opened not His mouth."
they slung accusations and hit Him
He was the son of GOD no doubt.
He has never left me destitute
He is still with me today,
I gave Him my word I'm votary
until I'm old and gray,
or till my mind evaporates
or I'm buried in the grave,
I cling to the hem of His garment
respectfully giving Him praise,
not even death can pry me away from Him
it's Him my heart adores,
although I love Him very much
He shows me He loves me more,
I am resolved to following JESUS
it is my duty everyday
He is worthy more than worthy
so I respectfully give Him praise . . .

He Knows What He Is Doing

Weeping may endure for a night
but joy comes on tomorrow
to relieve you of the stress you feel
and wipe away your sorrow
trouble doesn't last always
neither does your pain
although we go through problems here
someday we'll count it gain
sometimes the storm blows within our lives
and floods it with much rain
some people give up easily
something's are not explained
an earthquake sometime shakes us
to bring about a change
can't read GOD'S mysterious ways
sometimes His ways seem strange
we oft not know what's going on
but GOD always does
sometime He draws us nigh to Him
to envelope us with His love . . .

Nothing I Can't Acheive

There is a reason for my joy
no more frowns upon my face
by asking GOD for forgiveness
all my sins have been erased
He floods me with His mercy
saturates me with His grace
and the love He has towards me
is so pleasing to my taste
I can do all things through CHRIST
the one who strengthens me
by placing all my trust in GOD
there is nothing I can't achieve
there will be trials and trouble
someone hoping that I fall
so I turn my worship up
and give GOD my all in all
He watches over me
to make sure I make it through
He cleans my heart of all its dirt
to keep it pure and new
I can do all things
through CHRIST who strengthens me
as long as He is on my side there is nothing I can't achieve . . .

Workers Are Few

It doesn't matter what situation I am in
I have learned to be content
there is no need to mumble nor grumble
because time is so far spent
I am about my Father's business
there is much work I need to do
the harvest truly is plentiful
but the workers they are few
I stay prayed up and focused
keeping my eyes upon my goal
there are many who prevaricate
I'm just out to save one soul
people seem so busy
eager to sin they are bold
tomorrow is not promised
and the days are getting old
some people are flagitious
and those who refuse to listen
but when you close your eyes in death
there will definitely be a issue
then comes the JUDGMENT
you can't say you did not know
GOD will say depart from me
into eternity below
so I am about my Father's business
attending to His harvest
workers they are few
but sin has many artist . . .

Don't Get Caught

There is more to life than just here and now
this world is fading away
with humility I humble myself
and CHRIST I elevate
this life in which GOD has given me
I live day by day
I'm waiting upon His arrival
for I know He is on His way
I do not want to be caught partying
unrepentant while I sleep
He comes in the majesty of His glory
unexpectedly like a thief
I do not want to be caught in adultery
or coveting my neighbor's wife
or caught jesting and joking
or in the process of telling a lie
I do not want to be caught in war
trying to take someone else's life
I do not want to be caught doing wrong at all
when His word has taught me right . . .

Unafraid

I have lived in the ghetto
and I've seen the holds that keeps one trapped within
so no one can tell me about the ghetto
unless you have lived where I have been
such as renting an apartment
where a family of roaches reside
they come out to greet your company to bold to even hide
they are unafraid of roach spray
and live on pesticide
telling you to vacate their apartment
and they are unafraid to die
GOD lets us go through some things
to learn to appreciate what He provides
today I am thankful for all things
I'm so grateful to be alive
I look back a moment in time
and see how GOD'S blessings flow
and though I've lived once in the slum
it served to help me grow
the experiences that I've been through
today I apply to life
GODS way of speaking to me
motivates me to do what's right
I look back on that episode of roaches
where life continues to thrive
it doesn't matter what life sprays at me
in CHRIST I'm unafraid to die . . .

Hold Fast

From the troubles of earth to the joys of heaven
I'm rooted and grounded in CHRIST
my body sometimes feels the toil
but that's a part of life
I look towards heaven for my strength
to help me persevere
my mission is eternal life
so death I will not fear
I'm definitely sure there is better ahead
than what I'm going through now
until then I'll keep on pressing on
with both hands on the plow . . .

There Is A Cost

With precious blood I have been bought
this soul I have is not mine
so I must take care of it while I live
and return it when it's time
GOD will take it if it's good
if not He will turn it away
if right it will get a great reward
if not there is a price to pay
I admit this soul is not mine
instead it belongs to GOD
and upon return and inspection of it
I'll get paid for the labor I've wrought . . .

Jesus Service

In order to be a true soldier for CHRIST
armor up where ever you are
you will be attacked from satan on all fronts of life
and receive many battle scars
keep your mind open wherever you go
and be prepared to fight
keep on the whole armor of GOD
it will protect you through your plight
training always make better soldiers
'cause situations are sometimes tight
enroll today in JESUS' army
and keep fighting for eternal life . . .

Your Glory

Until I see Your glory
my life is in Your hands
until I've crossed this troubled land
been tried yet still I stand
until I see Your glory
my feet shall get no rest
because I want not the least reward
but I want the very best
until I see Your glory
can't afford myself be slack
for just as soon as I sit down
Your Son is coming back . . .

Vic'try Ground

Through JESUS CHRIST my Lord
I stand on vic'try ground
though opposition in many forms
sought to hold me down
attack my faith sneak in doubt
and drain my spirit dry
but I'll fight with everything I have
until it all subsides
today I stand a soldier
better prepared than ever before
I'm amazed to see the enemy go down
yet still come back for more
I've obtained many war wounds
which comes with any war
I've never been in any battle before
and come out without a scar
I am a veteran still at war
because I've refused to flee
I stand on vic'try ground
because CHRIST He strengthens me . . .

The Prisoner

The suffering of prisoners is so deep
their freedom has been taken
the worst fear in mind of them
is to be forgotten or forsaken
the aggression they endure
oft comes from cruel guards
they have contact with dangerous criminals
making matters even harder
their families suffer
some prisoners are heavy burdened
from the actions of their crime
and if someone else walked in their shoes
they probably would lose their mind
all have sinned and fallen short
from the beginning of their lives
some of us chose to repent
and strive to do what's right
remember always where you come from
and GOD isn't through with you yet
so He can also cleanse a prisoner up
and that don't ever forget . . .

A Book

What better gift to give at Christmas
than a book about JESUS CHRIST
which would last for many years
and touch so many lives
and remain a blessing long after Christmas
could lead to save a soul
and bring wisdom into someone's life
give blessings never told
so it's OK to shop around
but a book is always pleasant
the greatest joy one could receive
is JESUS as a Christmas present. GIVE A BOOK . . .

O' Death Where Is Thy Sting

O grave where is thy victory(1st cor. 15:55)
O death where is your sting
my hope lies in JESUS CHRIST
and all the joy He brings
I rejoice in His heavenly abode
and all the love to me He gives
CHRIST snatched the keys
to death and the grave
and rose that I might live
O grave where is thy victory
O death where is thy sting
you have no grip or hold on me
now I rejoice and sing . . .

A Heart Of Stone

Lord what a privilege to know
in this world You can use me
to go places and spread your word
to help someone believe
I'm glad to know You love me so
a man who has done much wrong
it's amazing to see You grow a beautiful tree
out of a heart of stone
out of all the sin I've committed
and made Your heart to grieve
I'm glad Your Son came and died
that I might be set free
it's amazing to know You love me so
and You direct my path
I'm grateful for Your sense of humor
bet I make you smile and laugh
I'm glad to know You love me so
a man who has done much wrong
it's amazing to see You grow a beautiful tree
out of a heart of stone . . .

Thick And Thin

When I was depressed you were there
to wipe away my tears
when I thought I could not make it
you helped me overcome my fears
when I needed help you were there
to give a helping hand
when I fell down you were there
and encouraged me to stand
when I would try your patience
you were there to show me love
you have many of GODS qualities
good people are really made of
I want to tell you that I love you
you are more than just a friend
you have been with me from the beginning
stuck by me through thick and thin
when I was in despair you picked me up
and lifted my spirit high
there have been times I've hurt your feelings
didn't mean to make you cry
I thank GOD for being the glue
that's held us together
though our relationship has seen some storms
you were there to make it better

cont -

I've made many mistakes
but experience has brought me through
and showed me how to make you happy
and taught me what not to do
I just want to thank you
for being more than just a friend
through the trouble and problems
throughout this life
you've stuck by me through
THICK AND THIN . . .

United Once Again

There is a day which I shall see
when all my struggles are gone
no more sorrow and no more grief
for I'll have made it home
JESUS saved me with His grace
He loves me and He cares
the greatest gift other than eternal life
would be to see my mother there
to know my family made it in
from all our awful sin
and all rejoicing in the LORD
united once again
I'll see my sister I've missed so much
and hug her with a grin
we'll be glad to see each other united once again . . .

Going Home

Think of closing your eyes
and waking up in paradise
think of laying down to rest
and being in heaven when you rise
think of noise in your ears
then all of a sudden peace
think of cotton candy land
where gold lays every street
think of celestial air
where nothing is ever wrong
can't wait for my visit to be over here
for there is no place like home . . .

Thank You

I thank GOD for sending you into my life
you mean the world to me
your encouragement lifted up my faith
and helped me to succeed
you believed I could do the impossible
when I was very low
your motivation helped me to believe
and helped my spirit grow
there is no limit in life to keep me bound
for now I'm free indeed
no words can express my gratitude
for all you've done for me
you medicated my mind with JESUS words
when I was weak within
you uplifted my spirit
revived my soul
I'm no longer compelled to sin
THANK YOU . . .

The School Of Life

In school there is a class
in which we hate to take
but in the school of life
some classes are hard
we must learn from our mistakes
sometime we must apply ourselves
instead of being late
sometimes the hardest classes
are actually those that turn out great
but if you learn any lesson
then the one you need to take is bible class
so you can learn life is what you make . . .

Jesus Rail

While sitting here thinking of you
and the wonderful times we had
thinking about when I would say something
and both of us would laugh
or taking a ride and you would yell
and say my driving was bad
or the times I would do something crazy
and you would get so mad
I wish the best for you today
and hope that all is well
I'm stronger than I've ever been
because I lean on JESUS RAIL
we separated for no reason at all
other than you needed space
so I withdrew from what I used to do
and let JESUS fill that space
but GOD gave me a glimpse of you
I hope your life goes well
but I'm stronger than I've ever been
as I lean on JESUS RAIL . . .

He's Not Finished

My life is just a portrait
that GOD hasn't finished yet
some would look at half the picture
make comments of regret
GOD views me from a distance
and knows that He's not through
but people view the painting unfinished
start judging and being rude
but the scene GOD paints next
is such a vital part
when if patient one would see it then
would have a change of heart . . .

Smiles Of Joy

You have often made mistakes in life
and some thought that you were done
you have often been entangled in sin
and trapped by the web you've spun
you've often had to retreat from sin
and often you have had to run
instead of facing certain defeat in life
you welcomed GOD to come
though GOD has truly changed your life
some day's for you are hard
but keep on pressing don't give up
though hope sometime seem far
life is fun, life is good
or should I say it's great
wouldn't trade one moment for anything
but cherish every day
CHRIST brings smiles of joy to life
death holds suffering and pain
CHRIST makes everything alright
and death wants life contained . . .

Be Nice

Remember those down trodden
and those in prisons and jail
because if the truth were known and told
many instances you could have fell
let He who is without sin cast the first stone
well how can you look down on them
when you're imprisoned in your home
be unafraid to entertain angels
for some have entertained angels unaware
if you want GOD to show you love
then show His people care . . .

Self Pride

The trouble with a self made man
is He worships His creator
self sits on the throne of His heart
and see no other greater . . .

We Are Unworthy

Just to live in this world
is beyond comprehension
because we are unworthy but been granted extension
GOD whose cup runs over with mercy
decided also to give us grace
we worship family and those we love down here
but GOD deserves our praise.
If we can humble ourselves and worship our kin
what about Him who forgives our sin
who came and died that we might live again
what better gift than eternal life from a friend . . .

Prayer Warrior

Prayer is like water for a tree
when it flows life manifests itself
when it ceases to flow leaves turn brown toward death
prayer is the mold in which Christians are shaped
it strengthens our heart and also faith
once prayer ceases hope fades
then we wander off life's path
and need a revival within our lives
and a serious spiritual bath
we can be restored because our roots aren't dead
but can die in a severe storm
so we need to keep prayer in our daily lives
to shield us from all harm . . .

A Heart Filled With Peace

Lord I thank you dearly for visiting me
while sitting in a jail
the most awful, lonesome, awakening experience,
in a 9 by 7 cell
it took all that to wake me up
through You my mind survived
resurrected my spirit
purified my heart and brought me back to life
then one day in the middle of praise
very gently You sent a breeze
and in that moment my life was changed
and my heart was filled with peace
I learned to walk, I learned to talk
I became born again
renewed my mind renewed my spirit
found joy that never ends
I'm no longer in trouble
life is beautiful
in JESUS I've found a friend
I've learned to deal with all life's terms
feels good to make amends
I bowed down and praised Your name
while crying on my knees
it was then that all my burdens were lifted
and my heart was filled with peace . . .

Jehovah Jireh—El Shaddai

Let no man say He has made me rich
only GOD only GOD alone
man didn't cause me to succeed
so His boasting leads Him wrong
man didn't cause me to achieve
nor save me but JESUS did
and He raised me up from among the dead
and all my sins He hid
man didn't cause me to survive
nor give me breath to stay alive
GOD has supplied all my needs
JEHOVAH JIREH—EL SHADDAI . . .

God Does Love You

Many people repeatedly experience
old pangs of guilt and hurt
they question how GOD could love them
when in their history is so much dirt
old sin can feel like glue
negative thoughts can also cling
so ask GOD to kindly remove them
then you can grow with great esteem
ones past can be so painful
looking back on situations
some even try to escape this
by changing habits and locations
some get depressed and down
looking sad and feeling blue
but if you search throughout the gospel
you will find GOD does love you
when you change your heart you can be liberated
from all that's gone before
like when JESUS told the lady caught in adultery
go and sin no more
the more you read and meditate
see what GOD has in store
the more you fast, the more you pray
will bring you nigh to heavens door
GOD DOES LOVE YOU . . .

A Brief Shadow

It's up to me to do what I will
with the life that I've been gave,
it's up to me to live right and do well
for I am not here to stay,
so I choose to follow JESUS
and be a servant to whom I can,
and though I face difficulties in life
He hasn't failed me still I stand,
life is a shadow of what's to come
the first go around is brief,
there is an eternal weight of glory to come
for those of us elite,
our faith must be tried by fire
to see if it dwindle or swell,
be careful not to think so highly of yourself
for some have stumbled and fell,
expect no reward while on this earth
for the duty in which you do,
have faith in the end you will win
for GOD will see you through,
life is a shadow of what's to come
the first go around is brief,
there is an eternal weight of glory to come
for those of us elite . . .

Worthless Art

when you pray
do you pray from the heart,
or do you create words of worthless art
do you mean what you say
when you speak to JEHOVAH,
or go through the motions
hurrying it to be over,
do you pray in vain
that others might see,
creative in thought
yet still don't believe,
are you a great artist
paint art that's untrue,
for pats on your back
for nothing you do . . .

Leave It With God

There's no need for you to worry
won't change a hair upon your head,
so just go down in prayer
and leave it with GOD instead,
there's no need for you to grumble
nor dwindle away with fret,
or get so sick you can not eat
from filled with so much dread,
so you just pray to GOD
and wait on Him to move,
for the battle is not yours
and that way you cannot lose,
trouble is not pleasant
whether small or whether big,
it will smack your husband
attack your wife
attempt to jump all on your kids,
but there's no need for you to worry
won't change a hair upon your head,
you just go down in prayer
and leave it with GOD instead . . .

You Can't Out Give God

Have you ever doubted GOD for something
and He blessed you
left you feeling numb,
He gave you a peep at His abundance
saying there's more where that come from,
the master steward is so unselfish
He knows what's best for me,
so I share from a caring spirit
it's better to give than to receive,
I've learned to praise and worship Him
in this brief little life I live,
I am the one who keeps taking from GOD
because it's GOD I can't out give,
it's all o:k when GOD comes through
and leave you amazed and stunned,
He gives a peep at His abundance
saying there's more where that come from . . .

The Sunset

As the sunset
so is this world about to end,
there will be a new heaven and a new earth
so a new birth need to begin,
we cannot be perfunctory
we must come with all our heart,
and strive with all the strength within
for evil must depart,
JESUS said (rev 22:20) "surely I come quickly"
so today is about to end,
it's important to give up our lives right now
so that we may live again,
His arms are wide open
He is extending to us His hug,
sure as the sun goes down
one day we will be judged . . .

Peace Be Still

In the midst of our storm
GOD is the only one who can say,
peace be still
and even the wind and waves obey,
today I put all my trust in Him
knowing He will make away,
He will lead and guide me and clear out paths
for me which are unknown,
cutting through wilderness and sticker briars
and breaking up hearts of stone,
He created everything magnificent
no flaws within His plan,
He gives me strength when I am weak
He gives me help so I can stand,
I will retire as a soldier
very militant for CHRIST,
the one who has all power
and gives eternal life,
though I walk through the valley of the shadow of death
I'll cling to JESUS hand,
the one who can make all quiet and still
by the voice of His command . . .

Accountable

I would rather spend the night in snow
than to be lost and go to hell,
I would rather do what JESUS wants
than do my will and yet it fail,
our life is based on choices
good choices reap good rewards,
all good and perfect gifts
come from one and that's the LORD,
life is not candy
every day will not be sweet,
even true some day's seem sour
what you sow is what you reap,
although I'm the most poetical
it's just talent on loan to me,
I can't brag nor can I boast
how I live is what you see,
I use this talent to gain interest
to partially pay my savior CHRIST,
so in the end when I do face Him
I'll obtain eternal life . . .

Goodbye . . . (Sympathy)

What I want to say
no words could ever express,
I always thought you would be there for me
I took life for granted I guess,
what I regret the most
and will forever make me cry,
is I didn't have a chance to say a final love you
or to say a last goodbye,
you were always my strength
any problem I had was yours,
I wish I could see that smile on your face
as you entered heavens doors,
we are never separated
even though we are apart,
you'll always be right here with me
in the center of my heart,
I'll always reminisce
and ask GOD the question why,
I love you and will see you again someday
but for now I say GOODBYE . . .

You Must Be Saved

Though you say you believe in JESUS
satan also believe and shakes,
doesn't matter what you believe in
can't get to heaven unless you're saved
(Romans 10:9-10)
(9) "if thou confess with thy mouth the LORD JESUS
and shalt believe in thine heart that GOD hath raised Him from the dead thou shalt be saved
(10) for with the heart man believeth unto righteousness
and with the mouth confession is made".
CONGRATULATIONS!! YOU ARE NOW SAVED.
(James 2:17) "faith without works is dead.
In this new life you have
live one moment at a time
you are now under the grace of GOD
who truly gives peace in mind . . .

Lifeguard

Although we get in deep
and seem we're going down
He's the one that watches o'er us
to make sure that we don't drown
(prov. 14:12) "there is a way that seemeth right unto a man
but the end thereof are the ways of death".
what look good isn't always good
and could be hazardous to your health,
satan is a master of deception
and will present you with gifts that's nice,
but the gift you think is so precious
may be nothing but just a vice,
something that will distract you
and leave you in His control,
He'll wait patiently for the opportunity
to try to steal your soul.
(EPH 5:12) "we wrestle not against flesh and blood
but against principalities against powers
against the rulers of the darkness".
Although we get in deep
and seem we're going down
He's the lifeguard who watches o'er us
to make sure that we don't drown . . .

True Humility

In all relationships trouble eventually comes around,
I've really tried my best though
to not ever let you down,
there is a time and place for everything
your feelings I didn't mean to crush,
I was unintentionally inconsiderate
and I got caught up in the rush,
if there are any consoling words
then they are hard to find,
cause I would definitely try to express them
to give you peace in mind,
I'm sorry I've let you down
some of my actions were not wise,
I'd like to say sincerely from my heart
that I APOLOGIZE.
GOD has been so good to us
and He deserve our thanks,
He picked us up when we were down
and thought that we would sank
every action bring consequence
and this we should expect
but in the heat of the moment
make the wrong decision
will bring you total regret

but if I could change the moment
then I more than eagerly would
and I wouldn't be facing embarrassment right now
but make everything all good
but life goes on one day at a time
I'll try regain your trust
I know it won't happen over night
I'm trying to make it like it was
I realize I've let you down
and my actions wasn't wise
I'd like to say sincerely from my heart
that I APOLOGIZE . . .

So Great

I want to take the timeout
and thank you for being such friend
and give all my gratitude
because on you I can depend
doesn't matter what problem
that I've been through
you were there with me to struggle
you have been by my side all through this life
when fate brought to me trouble
there's not one moment throughout my day
that I'm not thinking of you
you have been with me and shown me love
through all I've dreamed to do
GOD sends angels who has our back
so it is no mistake
that one who seems incredible
is truly so so great . . .

Sweet Sixteen

This is a day worth celebrating
a day beyond the norm,
a day in which I'm grateful for
the day that you were born,
so glad GOD placed you in my life
you mean so much to me,
I hope this day brings you great joy
for all eternity,
I know it seems you're aging fast
but it is just a dream,
and seems that years are zooming past
though 100 you feel 16,
I wish that I could be there now
and hug you with my arms,
but I'm away and could not make it today
so I sent instead this poem,
just to tell you not to panic
it's a day to be grateful for,
I hope that you're enjoying yourself
and I wish you many more. HAPPY BIRTHDAY!

Rest In Peace

Mother you are missed so very much,
I miss your hugs and special touch,
I miss your loving sweet tender ways,
grief brings to me such lonely days,
adjusting seems so very hard,
I can't repair my shattered heart,
I know you're in heaven with the LORD,
and many tears can't fill the void,
only GOD can take away my pain,
and place sunshine where there is rain,
one day real soon again we will meet,
until then I love you.
JUST REST IN PEACE . . . .

He Shines Through Me

There have been times that I've been down
didn't know just what to do,
I had no job I had to hustle
just to make it through,
there have been good times I chose to get dirty
to double my portion I had to grind,
trying to gamble to grow up big
in hopes one day that I might shine,
out of all that I have tried
vanity to no avail,
all the effort I applied
everything seemed still to fail,
BUT OH ! When I tried JESUS
and started to live within His gospel
is the day that I did grow
and in everything I prospered . . .

Children

Children oh children I'll have you know
there is more to life than rap,
many people have followed rappers to hell
another vice satan uses to trap,
if it's not positive then it's negative
with no middle ground between,
you're shown big money, sex, expensive cars
it's bait satan holds on a string,
many people buy CD's to hear lies told
that the rapper doesn't even live,
they like His jewelry and fancy clothes
which He buys with the money you give,
the only time you will see Him on a corner
will be His picture on a pole with a tack,
wanting you to pay $40.00 for a ticket
to come hear Him sing His tracks,
many rappers have sold their soul to satan
it's all apart of the game,
just to look big in front of the fans
for a moment of glory and fame,
children oh children I'll have you know
there is more to life than rap,
many people have followed rappers to hell
another vice satan uses to trap . . .

Double Minded

(JAMES 1:8)

There are a lot of two faced people
they blend in where ever they go,
they have no destination and are miserable inside
they have no logic which to take hold,
thy are unstable in all their ways
they are whom the bible call double minded,
one foot in life and one foot in the grave
they are the ones satan definitely has blinded,
they seek attention but are lacking love
so their path seem always dark,
only on Sunday they think of JESUS above
but He's never truly in their heart,
blessings and curses come out of their mouth
they forget the journey from whence they've came,
it's hard for them to grasp pure peace
for always dwelling on their past and pain,
they will be a christian on Sunday
and on Monday do dirt with no shame,
they always love the sunny days
but complain when storms bring rain . . .

Trials In Tribulations

Through experience that I have had in life
I know that trials will come,
but I am blessed even out of them
and know from whence they're from,
they are designed to strengthen my faith and walk
so when storms come I still stand,
and my feet be planted on solid ground
instead of sinking sand,
I've endured old man's vain traditions, silly intuitions
heard many contradictions,
and overcame satan's afflictions
I've closed my ears on gossip and conversations,
been through dangerous situations
one thing I know for sure to come is
TRIALS IN TRIBULATIONS . . . .

Jesus Hands

I just want to say hello
and ask you how you've been,
although you haven't heard from me in a while
I am still your friend,
I miss your lovely face and smile
and thought I'd send this poem,
to let you know you are not forgotten
but still in JESUS arms,
you're in my prayers day and night
I hope you are doing well,
although storms pop up in every ones life
I know you will prevail,
the hands that held nails once therein
now holds you safe and warm,
and comforts you within their grasp
while snuggled in His arms,
I just want to encourage you
keep striving do the best you can,
it's a great thing for me to know
that you are shielded in JESUS hands . . .

Talents

Man is made of flesh and bone
GOD gave us all a mind,
to know the difference between right and wrong
and a heart to be so kind,
what we do with what He gave
is up to one's own self,
flesh and bone goes back to dirt
but the soul proceeds our death . . .

Life After Death

Where the wind blows and also list
the sun will make a shadow,
trouble is forever dark
don't let your life be rattled,
when breath fades life's almost over
the world lights up again
this time it will shine forever
and joy will never end
I'll inquire within His temple
asking questions why and why,
for Him to answer He walked with me
through life's way by and by,
overflow I will embrace
and I will dine on it's increase,
no more angels fallen from heaven
finally there will be peace,
no more tears and no more sorrow
no more grief and no more pain,
because of JESUS who paid our cost
on that cross which He bloodstained . . .

Glory Beyond Compare

When all is done and said
there is a brighter side to see,
glory beyond compare
right there waiting for me,
not that I am worthy
nor for any deed I've done,
JESUS gave an invitation for salvation
accept it with works and come,
it is a lifetime job
in the end I will retire,
JESUS over came the world
through Him my works inspired,
so I live one day at a time
and be the best I can each day,
and witness to those who will listen
so my soul is worth it's stay,
glory beyond compare when I depart this earth
my soul will rejoice in heaven,
my flesh go back to dirt . . .

All In All

If I ever tried to stand alone
I am sure that I would fall,
that's why I cling to the son of GOD
He is my all in all,
He holds my hand so I won't stumble
and strengthens me when I am weak,
and when my flesh war against my spirit
He kindly gives me peace,
my intentions are to do good
though evil wants to steal my joy,
and lead me in another direction
with a decoy that will annoy,
so that's why I don't try to stand alone
I am sure that I would fall,
I place it all within JESUS hands
He is my all in all . . .

Nights To Days

Today my heart seem troubled
heavy with so much sorrow,
but my joy lies in the son of GOD
my hope for a better tomorrow,
though my day has seemed so dreary
my life has not grown dim,
I hold on to the grace of GOD
and place all faith in Him,
He has never let me down
He is a gift of gold to find,
He may not come when I want Him to
but He is always right on time,
we see only an image adumbrate of His grace
the best we haven't seen,
where day and night is always light
and grass is always green,
joy comes in the morning
tears won't last always
so hold on to GOD'S unchanging hands
He'll turn your nights to days . . .

He Is Real

"I sought the LORD and He heard me
and delivered me from all my fears".(psalm 34:4)
placed me back on solid ground
and wiped away my tears,
He showed me I was lacking faith
confidence I needed to build,
He touched my problem when my faith was low
to show me He is real . . .

Nothing

(Romans 8:35-39) "who shall separate us from the love of CHRIST?
Shall tribulation or distress or persecution or famine or nakedness
or peril or sword?
As it is written, for thy sake we are killed all the day long;
we are accounted as sheep for the slaughter
Nay, in all these things we are more than conquerors
through Him that loved us.
For I am persuaded that neither death, nor life, nor angels,
principalities, nor powers, nor things present, nor things to come, nor
height, nor depth, nor any other creature, shall be able to separate us
from the love of GOD which is in CHRIST JESUS our LORD".
Not father, not mother, not sister or brother, not husband, not wife
or any other not governments, nor money, or sugar, or honey
nor children, or land, neither can satan pluck us out of JESUS hand.
NOTHING! Will be able to separate me from the love of GOD . . .

Endless Rain

Sometime it seem you're drowning
from all the drenching rain,
the storms that blow into your life
leave scars from all the pain,
you're sometimes caught without protection
your spirit gets thoroughly wet,
through the clouds you hope to see the sun
to dry up all the fret,
GOD knows your every need
and the peace in which you hunger,
the rain that blows into your life
only makes you stronger,
seem when it rain it pours
and your problems are never slack,
you long to see the sun shine through
and soon your clouds will crack,
satan tries to over whelm you
so He attacks you with a mizzle,
and when He sees that that is not enough
He hits you with a drizzle,
GOD knows that you love Him
He gives the peace in which you hunger,
the endless rain that is in your life
will only make you stronger . . .

Wake Up O' World

Wake up o' world
oh what a beautiful day,
wake up give GOD some glory
for He is worthy to be praised,
the mountains sing hallelujah
and clouds smile up above,
all radiating the magnificence of GOD
and all His wonderful love,
WAKE UP! WAKE UP O' WORLD
give GOD His praises due,
the flowers look towards heaven
and birds sing about His truth,
so let us look towards heaven
while absorbing His beautiful grace,
and bask within His mercy
a sweet forever taste,
wake up you sleepy world
and open wide your eyes,
let us lift to Him our worship
we are the most blessed of all His prize . . .

Watch And See

Son though you feel forsaken
I want you to know that I do care,
the trial that you are going through now
is to strengthen you but I am always there,
I hear the question in your prayers
no I've never turned my back,
my will is to keep you focused
so you do not become distracted,
the place in which I'm taking you
you do not know the way,
so I have to hold your hand and guide your steps
each and everyday,
satan wants to destroy you
sift you just like wheat,
so I have to protect you from all harm
even as I speak,
I have to nudge you in the right direction
until you become firm and strong,
and is able to walk on your own
and do right instead of wrong,
you need to honor me give me glory
bow down to the ground prostrate,
worship me and give me praise
acknowledge me in all your ways,
I am making you strengthen your faith
so without question you will believe,
may not come when you want me to
but right on time you watch and see.

More Than Able

GOD thank you for another day
I'm living to see go by,
my spirit was feeling kind of low
but you have lifted me up high,
and though today's been trying
eternal life I still pursue,
and what satan meant to hinder me
has only helped me through,
when I struggle I know you are by side
and everything's ok,
when I invited you into my life
you entered my heart to stay,
I know you are more than able
to turn gray clouds into blue,
and part the clouds asunder
and let the sunshine through,
I know you're more than able
to pick me up if I should fall,
and give my spirit a boost
when it's weary and bout to stall,
I know you're like Tylenol
you provide me extra strength,
and LORD I'm very thankful
to know you'll go to any length,
in the presence of my enemies
you prepare for me a table,
any area that I'm lacking in you are more than able . . .

Thy Word

"Thy word is a lamp unto my feet
and a light unto my path".(psalm 119:105)
"Thy word have I hid in my heart
that I might not sin against thee".(psalm 119:11)
your word comes to my memory when I am in need
assisting me in inviting others to your throne.
(Hebrews 4:12) "It is quick and powerful, and sharper than
any two edged sword and cuts between right and wrong".
It is a wonderful help when I need comfort
it gives me peace and hope,
it helps me deal with all types of people
and gives me strength to cope,
it is the road map that leads to heaven
the only road that goes that away,
it teaches me how to live like CHRIST
and the image I ought portray . . .

Amazing Marvel

A wise man knows how little He knows
truth leads to the vast ocean of knowledge
whose depths just can't be measured,
a fool says there is no GOD
and squanders life with pleasure,
marvel grows greatly when knowledge increases
curiosity is good for the brain it pleases,
true knowledge contains the whole being
the heart, the spirit, and soul,
wisdom is a jewel one should adorn
ignorance is a fool hard to hold,
what good is knowledge if you don't use it
it's like the brain collecting dust,
what good is knowledge that has no substance
or a heart that's made like crust,
what good is a thought that contains no love
and reveals only it's lust
what good is your life if you let your soul burn forever
knowing your flesh returns back to dust . . .

Again And Again

I've flapped my wings but still haven't flown
but with CHRIST I know I'll soar,
I haven't scratched the surface yet
of all He's got in store,
in His hand there is a blessing
meant especially for me,
all I have to do is obey
have faith and just receive,
I've seen Him work and He's marvelous,
His love will never end,
and right when I'm content with what I have
He blesses me again,
He fills my cup with awe
He's worthy to be praised,
so I honor and acknowledge Him
in all of my ways
I've seen His work He's marvelous
His love will never end,
and right when I'm content with what I have
He blesses me again . . .

Overcast

The odds were stacked against me
my heart felt really troubled,
seemed there was no one there to help me
nor any arms in which to cuddle,
my resume appeared so dreary
clouds of trials the overcast,
some say time heals all wounds
LORD I wish that these would past,
GOD knows more than me
so there's no need to wear a mask,
GOD is willing to forgive me
people forgiving a harder task,
only GOD can build an overpass
until then I still pray,
I long to see the sun to shine
right now the clouds seem gray,
my hope it is in JESUS
there is a better day ahead,
so my praise I lift unto my GOD
and ask for peace instead,
I know He will remove the contrast
that make the clouds seem gray,
and remove my burden far from me
cause trouble don't last always . . .

My Help

GOD has been so good to me
better than I've been to myself,
when I thought I couldn't make it through
GOD was there to help,
and when I felt so alone inside
He came and brought me peace,
and comforted me within myself
and put my spirit at ease,
the storms that's come into my life
GOD has brought me through,
and when I've felt so torn inside
He restored my soul a new,
today GOD has been so good to me
better than I've been to myself,
and when I thought I couldn't make it through
GOD was there to help . . .

"Faith In Him"

ALL things are possible with faith
just believe and it is so
JESUS He will make away,
there is a bright and sunny side
when life on earth seem dull,
when our daily life inside this shell
appears to be so null,
but when we let go and then let GOD
direct our pathway straight,
and watch what He's doing in our life
in building up our faith,
yes problems will come
some days will seem bleak and dim,
but by experience everything will be alright
when we have faith in Him . . .

What You Sow

AS you are planting your garden
put in the best of your seed,
because what you sow
that definitely you will also reap,
the same it is with life
some often sow bad seed,
and expect good to come of it
but are surprised at what they reap,
today the harvest is ready
the question is what have you sown?
Nothing bad comes out of good
the seed reveals what you have grown,
start today planting good seed
spread it at the saviors throne,
He will fertilize it and give increase
and bless the seed that you have thrown . . .

Hope

"The things which happened unto me
have fallen out rather unto the furtherance of the gospel".
GOD does everything for a reason
to make us stronger ones
we must go through life' trials to triumph
and have victory through His son
so when life seem so burdensome
and you are staring at despair
is when He makes the best out of a bad situation
to let us know that He is there
experience strengthens our testimony
and can be a gift that you can't see
but is a blessing to someone else heart
so that they can be set free
so take the bitter with the sweet
and use it all for JESUS CHRIST
what you are going through right now
maybe hope in someone's life . . .

Good Growth

Daily we need to extirpate our thinking
get rid of hindering thoughts
the HOLYSPIRIT can lead us then
help us walk the way we ought
and be kind one towards another
refrain from being quick to blame
look in the mirror and take a look at our own self
and be the christian that most of us claim
without love it's impossible to know CHRIST
who died to set us free
so let go of all your resentments
because they stack up to much grief
get rid of pride and ego
JESUS will get rid of your woe
knowledge is the key to success
the way your spirit will grow . . .

It Could Be Worse

Today your life feels pressured
as your burdens weigh you down,
and your mind is in despair
and your troubles hold you bound,
but though your faith is tried
thank GOD it could be worse,
and praise His holy name always
cause in your life He does come first,
there's others more unfortunate than you
so you kneel and pray for them,
though sometime your mind feel grief
their lives are grim and dim,
there is nothing you can't overcome
praise GOD for His dear son,
though satan wants your mind to doubt
CHRIST overcame this world and won,
and still you haven't gotten what you deserve
thank GOD it could be worse,
and praise His holy name because, in your life He does come first . . .

God has never

When life is overbearing sometimes
and problems won't go away,
and the sun won't shine in your life
and clouds seem always gray,
seems GOD won't listen when you pray
and hope is dwindling slim,
GOD has never turned His back on us
but we have turned our backs on Him,
in trouble we wonder why we hurt
and suffer from so much pain,
but in good times we are happy with smiles
some live this life in vain,
we need to reevaluate life
when the storms in life seem dim,
GOD has never turned His back on us
but we have turned our backs on Him . . .

Accept His Love

In spite of circumstances
don't let trouble hold you down,
life sometime seem grim
as problems seek to hold you bound,
do not rely upon yourself
look towards JESUS for your help,
and let Him direct your path
His guidance be sure to accept,
in this old troubled world down here
GOD is due glory and all praise,
He has put up with us ever so long
still some rebel His ways,
He keeps this world so maintained
also tends to you and me,
GOD never wants us bound up but free as an autumn breeze,
and if He waters His big trees how much more will He do for us
He will pour out a blessing you want have room to receive
nor room for you to store . . .

I'm So Proud

As I sit and think of your innocence
and the joyful times we've had,
I can't think of anything more precious than you
I'm so proud to be your dad,
you will realize time goes quickly
one day you will soon be grown,
you can always talk to me about anything
long as I have a house you've got a home,
if you need to talk about a problem
or you feel someone has done you wrong,
you can always bring it to me
you have a shoulder in which to lean on,
If life feels overbearing and you think all hope is gone,
I'll be a phone call away
I'll be your strength until you're strong,
as I sit and reminisce
of the joyful times we've had,
GOD truly has blessed us with each other
and I'm so proud to be your dad . . .

Get A Grip

All we need is to get a grip
on this busy world unkind,
look towards the hills
from whence cometh our help,
leave all our stress behind
GOD uses rain sometime,
to cleanse the world below
if GOD should turn His back on us,
then whither shall we go
His cup runneth over with mercy,
He has extended to us His grace
some think tomorrow is promised,
and do not seek the Savior's face
cars going back and forth,
planes perturbing the air
people have no love for one another,
seems many do not even care
JESUS will come when all least expect it,
so get your temple in order
so upon accounting on judgment day,
you won't be there just to loiter. GET A GRIP . . .

Love One Another

"A new commandment I give unto ye that ye love one another;
as I have loved ye, that ye also love one another."
Every person in this world is related
whether you want to be or not,
so all the hating and discriminating
you need repent right now and stop,
because GOD won't bless no mess
and you cannot be GOD,
so come unto GOD and quit judging
repent right now and stop,
let not your heart be troubled
weighed down with rotten fruit,
do unto others as yourself
the way you would have others do back to you,
let not your heart be troubled
face it everything you do not know,
If you are looking down on another brother
it's hard for you to grow,
it is best to pray to GOD
ask Him to change your ways,
bless your heart bless your mind
and He will bless your days,
everyone in this world is related
from the beginning up to this day,
if you are harboring bad fruit within your heart
repent right now and pray . . .

God Will Bring You Out

Are you in the wilderness
doing divers kinds of sin,
rebelling against the way of GOD
being hard and will not bend,
some things we must experience
to learn not to take that route,
that's the way GOD sometime restore us
to bring a change about,
experience builds our character
through weakness we are made strong,
GOD has ways to get our attention
to show us right from wrong,
sometimes He must chastise us
to bring us nigh to Him,
but there is light at the end of the tunnel
when the road you're traveling is dim,
GOD will bring you through
when you surrender to Him your will,
when the road you are on keeps winding
and the journey seems all up hill,
He will take away despair
and your spirit He will renew
when you look towards JESUS for all your help
GOD will bring you through . . .

Lost

What's ahead the godless cannot see
they ponder death with fear,
forever seeing but still cannot perceive
forever hearing but yet to hear,
they live in the moment having fun right now
hoping their party will never end,
instead of following JESUS to eternal life
they chose to follow death with trends,
JESUS was tempted just as we are
yet still overcame this world,
some people don't even try to prevail
it's like tossing swine our precious pearl,
"Every knee will bow and every tongue will confess
that JESUS CHRIST is LORD".(Philippians 2:10-11)
that will be a day that all is in agreement
by witness all on one accord,
before you continue to shut out JESUS
calculate the cost,
though you think you have found your way in this life
are you in the wilderness lost . . .

Priceless Pearl

Stand up be a man of GOD
don't let satan lead you astray,
in order to be a good Christian
let go of your evil desires
because CHRIST did not act that away,
you are holding onto the sin that easily beset you
and makes you a slave to this world,
you can fool man some of the time
but you can never fool our priceless pearl . . .

Reality Check

Sometime we need to revisit the hardship
for reality to stare us in the face,
for us to realize that there is a GOD
to learn to cherish breathing,
to learn life is not to waste
to learn we can't count our blessings,
to overlook the problems around
He has shown much mercy throughout our lives,
so life is not to regret
sometime we need to revisit hardship,
to receive a reality check . . .

I Am Anchored

When all my labors and trials are overbearing
I will get my just reward,
bow down in front of my Saviors feet
give Him honor and regard,
till then I'll keep on trudging
to satan I am a rancor,
though storm's sometimes blow on me
in JESUS CHRIST I am anchored,
no one told me life was easy and trials I do not regret,
CHRIST was tempted just as we are
and Him I give utmost respect,
He overcame this world so it is not impossible
he showed me that it could be done,
if I labor and take my eyes off this world
and stay focused on Him the Son,
sometime I must go through the valley
satan looks like a rancor
though the storms of life beat on me sometimes
in JESUS CHRIST I'm anchored . . .

Fire Shut Up In My Bones

Be not weary in well doing
this is our reasonable service to GOD,
we will reap if we faint not
stay determined and continue to plod,
thank you LORD for not giving up on me
that motivates me even more to keep on,
thank you for your mercy and your grace
and for blessing me with strength to stay strong,
thank you for giving me your yoke
your burden is ever so light,
thank you for your HOLY SPIRIT
which takes me to marvelous heights,
It's like fire shut up in my bones
a feeling worth total surrender,
GOD you are way beyond reliable
your work amazing splendor . . .

Life Doesn't Stop

We never stop living
after we depart from here,
you need to worry about your salvation
with much trembling and fear,
all of our righteousness
will not add up to enough,
it's through GOD'S mercy and grace
that we are sustained by His love,
life goes on
there is a better life after death,
we need to set an example of good
and worry about our soul and not about self,
it's easy to get tangled up
and bound in fetters by sin,
when we take our eyes off JESUS CHRIST
who made it possible to live again,
if His eye is on the sparrow
then I know He watches me,
if He keeps them from falling
how much more He catches me,
I may not have what I always want
but He provides all my needs,
I hold on to His unchanging love
in Him I trust and believe . . .

My Strength

It was there in the midst of my darkest times
I prayed within the dark,
was then when my faith was low
deeply troubled in my heart,
but through the storms that rained on me
GOD kept me safe and dry,
and let the sunshine into my life
and told me not to cry,
He revealed to me that He was real
and showed me with His signs,
though satan wanted me to doubt
GOD almost blew my mind,
right when I felt like giving up is when my LORD came through,
He strengthened me beyond compare
and helped my life regroup . . .

Nails In My Testimony

Raised below poverty
more mud than grass,
where many had no manners
let alone any class,
young and in trouble
my world began to spin,
many days I would hope
that life would come to an end,
we had to go to church
but that wasn't enough,
it was years before I found JESUS
after problems got tough,
searching for happiness in the wrong places
I found the wrong street
and started using drugs,
no one told me life was easy
and I thought that it was fair,
only to find out very quickly
sometimes it's rocky with despair,
but through all my living
GOD showed me He cared,
just nails in my testimony
to show that He had been there . . .

It's Going To Be Alright

Joy comes in the morning
after weeping all through the night,
where as it seemed there is no hope
in the distance there is a light,
there will always be problems
long as this ol' world exist,
so you need to be prayed and fasted up
have wit about satans tricks,
don't stay down if you get hit
from something that feels like a knife,
get up and just keep fighting on
it's going to be alright,
trying times build spiritual muscle
GOD has angels all about,
doesn't matter what you are going through
GOD can bring you out,
even if you're bound by vices
GOD can give release,
and fill the void occupied
restore your heart with peace,
so don't stay down
although you're hit by something that feels like knife
get up and just keep fighting on
it is going to be alright . . .

Your Help

What better time to praise the LORD
Than when trouble has bound you tight,
that's when GOD will give you peace and joy
to know everythings alright,
in spite of trouble on the front
GOD has got your back,
I have never seen sincerity forsaken
and that's a proven fact,
look towards heaven for relief
do not rely on self,
turn all your problems over to CHRIST
and He will be your help,
satan will make you feel guilty
for failing GOD with promises before,
but today is the day of salvation
so go ahead and knock on JESUS door,
His cup runneth over with mercy
He will deliver you once more,
just strive to do the will of GOD
and see what that has in store,
look towards heaven for relief
do not rely on self,
turn all your problems over to GOD
and He will be your help . . .

I Love To Sing Him Praise

There is a name I love to hear
I love to sing Him praise,
He floods my heart with tremendous joy
He brightens up my days,
through trouble pain and turmoil
my soul is full of peace,
I'll praise the lord til my mind is gone
or this life has come to cease,
I constantly watch and pray
cause satan tries to plunder,
destroy my life and steal my soul
keep me and GOD asunder,
there is a name I love to hear
He brightens up my days,
He floods my heart with tremendous joy
I love to sing Him praise . . .

Still I Stand

In spite of all that come against me
I will honor and praise your name,
satan tries to inflict me
with temptation trials and pain,
He always come against me
He's a thorn deep in my flesh,
because I am sold out to you LORD
He doesn't ever let me rest,
He's very busy in this world
seeking whom He can devour,
but through your strength I stand steadfast
He can never defeat your power,
weeping may endure for a night
but there is joy at the end of pain,
I like to triumph over sorrow
and smile though yet it rain,
I am a witness to your fame
cleansed my temple from all it's stain,
I glorify your holy name
through JESUS CHRIST I am ordained,
if I slip and I stumble I am stabled by your hand
your grace is so sufficient,
through it all still I stand . . .

God Is Awesome

It is amazing to see dew on the grass
and view the rolling hills,
to see GOD water His big trees
see bee's on daffodils,
to hear the rooster crow on time
cows moo in country fields,
to have deep peace in time of trouble
and know that GOD is real,
to smell fatback early in the morn
and chew the crispy rinds,
to hear a neighbor say hello
and enjoy the southern kind,
to enjoy pork chops with hot sauce
cornbread and collard greens,
or to enjoy peace and quiet
fishing serene in a silent stream,
there is nothing like bacon grease
fried right along with cabbage,
to rock in a rocker on the porch
while glancing at a feasting rabbit,
to view Carolina mountains in the fall
amazed at the beautiful leaves,
to glance the expanse from the blue ridge parkway
really puts one mind at ease,
GOD is awesome!GOD is awesome!
There's no comparison to Him,
He created the french broad river
it's full of catfish, bass and brim . . .

No Other Help I Know

It feels heavy for me to pray
submit to you my request,
all the mercy that you've given me
I am truly blessed,
no other help I know in the heavens or on the earth
that I can call upon for help that is alive and still at work,
one who controls the wind
and makes the ocean roar,
one who makes the sun to shine
and illuminates the stars,
one who speaks like thunder
and replenish the earth with rain,
one who has the power in His hand
to take away my pain,
I come humbly to your throne
submitting my request to you above,
thank you GOD for finding favor in me
and for blessing me with your love . . .

We Are Waiting

Help us father not to succumb to trials
give us strength to endure to go that extra mile,
give us energy to not give up when the road appears uphill,
when our journey seem lonely we have blessed assurance
that you are guiding us still,
this world is getting older as we wait upon our savior,
to bring from heaven to earth His glory and give to us His favor . . .

The Source

(John 14:1-4)
"Let not your heart be troubled;
ye believe in GOD, believe also in me.
In my fathers house are many mansions:
if it were not so I would have told you
I go to prepare a place for you,
and if I go to prepare a place for you
I will come again and receive you unto myself;
That where I am, there you maybe also
and whither I go ye know, and the way ye know."
I look forward to closing my eyes
knowing that my labor is not in vain,
If CHRIST said it He meant it He cannot lie
no more tears and no more pain,
our goal should be to love one another
and do the job He left us to do,
the good work He started in us He will finish
He promised He would see it through.
(proverb 18:24) "There is a friend who sticks closer than a brother."
You can search but won't find one greater
the author and finisher of our faith
a loving and merciful creator,
some look at me and wonder
what reason is there to rejoice,
I've got joy and peace inside of me
JESUS He is the source . . .

O' Happy Day

I thank you GOD for your beautiful days
I thank you GOD for accepting my praise,
I thank you GOD for hearing my prayer
I thank you GOD you are always there,
I can talk to you about anything
just as your birds which chirp and sing,
just as your grass is rich and green
you are my stanchion on which I lean,
you play sweet notes upon my ears
which no one else seem even hear,
my soul was purchased sold with receipt
I thank you LORD for valuing me,
I love you as much as a horse loves hay. O'happy day O' happy day . . .

My Stanchion

I cast my burdens upon you LORD
to much for me to bear,
I know for sure you will tend to them
like you do my every care,
without your loving hand in place
I would have no hope at all,
without you holding me up most often
oh most definitely I would fall,
when I was unstable you steadied me
you quenched my every fear,
you made my sorrows disappear
and wiped away my tears,
you've blessed my life time after time
most often undeserved,
you've showed me to not think highly of myself
to be a drudge be humble and serve . . .

There Is No Excuse

Work while it is day
for the night cometh when no man can work,
it is important to train the laymen of the church
through many people long since gone,
GOD'S gracious providence has shone
and left a path to lead us home,
there is no excuse for us going wrong
do nothing that you ought not be doing when JESUS come,
go no place where you
would not like to be found when He returns,
be GODLY and humble in all you do
and in all you do still stand firm,
all that needed to be done
was done right on the cross,
there is no excuse for man living to die
and let His soul be lost . . .

Death Will Have No Hold

For sin shall not have dominion over me
for I am not under law but under grace,
so shall I continue in sin, GOD forbid
I am living now to live again,
everyday that I awake
with satan I am in affray,
every time He brawls with me He leaves disappointed
there is nothing here for Him to take,
sometime I get tired and weary
each day this flesh gets old,
one day I'll close my eyes appear to sleep forever
but death will have no hold . . .

Give

It is better to give than receive,
for GOD said He would allow men to give back into your bosom
good measure, pressed down, running over
that's a promise which you can believe,
so do not be hesitant to be of service to someone
be sure to do your most,
deny yourself and follow the lead
as you are led by the HOLY GHOST,
and praise GOD that He allowed you
to serve and be of help,
don't be selfish and inconsiderate
nor think too highly of yourself. GIVE . . .

This Too Shall Pass

Out of all the wrongs I've done in life
GOD'S patience is oh so real,
I've done nothing to deserve His grace
but yet He loves me still,
although trials attack my faith
and seems much is on my plate,
my problems seem much a task
but I'll just sit and pray and wait,
I seek the LORD sometime
it seem to no avail,
doubt attacks my spirit
and leaves my hope so frail,
tears flow so steady
I lose my breath can't inhale,
sometime I feel like giving up and crying and say oh well,
I look back see how far GOD'S brought me
through such a rugged trail,
it seem dark and dreary in life sometime but never will it last
I know my mountain has to level off—this problem too shall pass . . .

Renew Within Me A Right Spirit

It's good to constantly review your thoughts
to see what's happening within your mind,
because our brain sometime wander off
most often to thoughts unkind,
the subconscious entice our spirit
which can jeopardize the soul,
sometime we entertain ideas
that are so unwise to hold,
daily I pray to GOD
To renew the HOLY SPIRIT within,
and to cast out anything ungodly
never to return again,
who am I but only human
sometimes I make mistakes,
I look towards the hill
from whence cometh my help,
to keep my pathway straight
so when my mind try wander off,
GOD puts me back on track
and renew within me a right spirit,
so that I don't go back . . .

A Yearning Heart

He felt more pain in His heart
than He did upon His skin,
all the holes in His body He wore
were nothing compared to our sins,
pontius Pilate was very dissolute
He was only fulfilling scripture,
I would love to see His face when He faces JESUS
Kodak a moment with His picture,
the world sat still a moment stunned
continuing to plot their madness,
but those who saw and recognized Him
got bold and preached with gladness,
there is reason for joy so do rejoice
His remnant is still here,
when He comes there will be no divulsion apart
nor either a spirit of fear . . .

Angels

Angels are ministering spirits sent forth to serve
for the sake of some to obtain salvation,
angels are beings sent by GOD
to help us in certain situations,
so do not be afraid to entertain strangers
for thereby some have entertained angels unaware,
(True story) I remember traveling from Ohio to north Carolina
one year I caught a flat and had no spare,
when a Cadillac pulled up and asked if it could help
I said yes turned around for a moment looked back and was alone
the Cadillac was gone, 3o minutes later a tow truck came
and fixed my tire said a person in a Cadillac awaits me at the gas
station had no money to pay for the new tire, babies in the car
rain coming down heavy as I followed the tow truck there.
As we pulled up to the gas station a person came out
held out their hand and gave me a $50.00 bill.
GOD knew I had a long way to go couldn't have made it by myself,
so GOD sent a ministering angel from heaven there
just to bring me help . . .

Sleepy Head

Wake up now it's time to arise
above all darkness and satan's lies,
my GOD my GOD! Oh what a surprise
the ones that slumbered have opened their eyes,
no weapon satan has will be able to prosper
only peace will prevail and the truth of the gospel,
victory is the LORD'S surprise surprise
those who slumbered have opened their eyes . . .

The Battle Is Gods

Let the battle be GODS
in your time of a struggle,
let His strength be exhibited
just rely on His muscle,
do all things through CHRIST
who gives you your strength,
doesn't matter what depth nor length or width
GOD will deliver you through trouble,
and help you prevail
though satan attack,
you still will excel
the battle is not ours it belongs to GOD
when we go it alone we are against the odds . . .

No Other Help I Know

Besides my GOD and my JESUS
no other help do I know,
beyond the magnificent heaven
nor earth or below,
it doesn't matter what hour
His throne I can go,
He just speaks to my problems
and away they do blow,
I've searched there is none
with power like His
who creates worlds
so vast and so big
who controls the wind
and directs the sea
there's no other help I know
that is sufficient for me . . .

Be Kind

It is better to give others a piece of your heart
than to give them a piece of your mind,
it is easier to lead someone who is lost
by showing love and being so kind . . .

I Am Yours

Search deep in me for any hidden sin
and find my heart is pure,
For I am only human flesh
LORD help me to endure,
you see and know what I do not
I am a child of yours,
you guide me in my daily walk
and open up my doors,
though sometime I walk into a storm
seem when it rain it pours,
I thank you LORD for your sunshine
I am a child of yours . . .

The Decision Of Your Life

To be absent from the body is to be present with CHRIST
so of death you should be unafraid,
GOD keeps us in His best interest
even during times when we have strayed,
He wants none of us to perish
but stay in the presence of His love,
don't let your mind be dormant
learn and come to know life,
and know to be absent from the body will not mean death
but to be present with JESUS CHRIST,
there is life after death
but I wish no soul to go,
where there is torment and gnashing of teeth
in a place that's named Sheol,
for those who sin and disobey
this will be your home,
here you'll spend eternal life
and pay for all your wrongs,
the decision of life is yours
after death life goes on,
so what you choose right now upon this earth
will decide your future home . . .

Brighter Side

Of all the things I've suffered here
I can't boast nor boost my pride,
I count my trials and temptations joy
for I know there's a brighter side,
through all the problems, trouble and trials
my face still hold a smile,
knowing my labor is not in vain
I keep pressing for another mile,
I walk step by step take day by day
for there's a brighter side,
who am I but what GOD created
His servant until the end,
though it seem sometime I am in a storm
I won't quit, submit, nor give in,
though weeping endureth for a night
I know GOD'S love is wide,
so in spite of all my circumstances
there is a brighter side . . .

Sit Still

We need to ask GOD to go with us
and never go it alone,
that way we have life insurance
that's how we don't go wrong,
some questions we have no answer to
concerning the hand that life has dealt,
but GOD is always there for us
an ever present help,
He knows our every thought
and exactly how we feel,
sometime we need to let Him work
be patient and just sit still,
if we remove ourselves out of the way
and watch the LORD at work,
He will restore us to the fullest measure
and bandage up our hurts,
if you hold on a little longer
GOD will be revealed,
there is no doubt that He is real
so be patient and just sit still . . .

A Beautiful Piece Of Art

The foundation of ones soul
needs an elevator to the roof of happiness,
then we will see in depth our imagination
GOD will reveal what we do not know,
if we search from the soul with an open mind
and hold on to His unchanging hand,
and not walk as one who is blind
and be willing to grow beyond the norm,
instead of being miserable in the land of unhappiness
the foundation of ones soul is where it begins,
in order to build towards eternal life
initial life causes no harm,
but the vices we create assuredly will
the spiritual side is the deepest side of ones heart,
GOD created a beautiful piece of art . . .

Trouble Won't Last Always

Life is full of drama
sometime bring cloudy days,
in spite of all our circumstances
we still owe GOD our praise,
He knows just what is best for us
and wants us to obey,
like rain always tapers off
trouble want last always,
like sheep we sometime go astray
sin doesn't never pay,
it often brings us misery
and many dreary days,
but thanks be to JESUS
who conquered death and the grave,
in all points tempted just as we are
so trouble won't last always,
He leads us to green pasture
and lets us freely graze,
do not bite the hand that feed you
Him we shouldn't betray,
we are only here temporary
we are not here to stay,
so treat today like it's your last day
live right and continuously pray,
once you have tasted the goodness of JESUS
in your heart there should be a crave,
in your spirit He will place a peace so deep
you'll know trouble won't last always . . .

Tomorrow Isn't Promised

There exist pleasure and entertainment
then comes judgment and sorrow,
today is the day of salvation
we just can't wait until tomorrow,
look in the mirror and start judging
dig deep within be honest,
a lil talk with JESUS can make it right
for tomorrow is just not promised,
today is like the days of Noah
people are to busy for the LORD,
separation is very popular
only a few on one accord,
JESUS laid down His life so that we may cross His bridge,
His blood cleanses us from all unrighteousness
doesn't matter what you've did,
so look in the mirror and start judging
dig deep within be honest,
just a lil talk with JESUS can make it right
for tomorrow is just not promised . . .

Missing You

I miss you very much
you're always on my mind,
as I think of the great moments we've had
and all our wonderful times,
I miss talking with you
about most anything,
I miss all the joy and happiness
in my life you used to bring,
I miss us cooking out
putting hotdogs on the grill,
just to be within your presence
I considered it a thrill,
you're in the center of my heart
your memories are vivid strong,
you watched as I became a man
you taught me right from wrong,
I know you're up in heaven
looking down upon me now,
it's your spirit sometimes that's guiding me
and tells me when and how,
though gone you live within our hearts
you're where GOD'S love keeps you warm,
no more sickness there within that land
you're safe in JESUS arms
we miss you . . .

No More

I know it seems lately
storms has brought much rain,
but hold on we are working on a heavenly reward
of no more sorrow and no more pain,
there are better days
but we must remain strong,
trials don't last always
tomorrow they will be gone,
so we must keep trudging alone
doing right instead of wrong,
pray in spite of your circumstances
in your spirit just sing a song,
and be thankful for all things
blessings will leave you awed,
our hearts sometime need forgiveness
from the damage which satan has gnawed,
sometime we are not balanced
we trip over obstacles and stumble,
we must learn a lesson from our troubled past
to keep us grounded and humble,
I know it seem lately storms has brought much rain
but hold on we're working on an heavenly reward
of no more sorrow no more pain . . .

Stronger Than Ever

How do you keep your eyes on JESUS
when they are full of tears,
how do you stay focused
when you realize your fears are real,
do not be troubled by trouble
continue to do what's right,
do not doubt in the dark
what GOD has showed you in the light,
it is hard to stay focused
when it appears GOD is not there,
GOD knows our every step
and hears our every prayer,
we must last throughout the storm
though we get drenched from all it's rain,
even when it seem our prayers fall short
and we are praying to Him in vain,
He said He would not leave nor forsake us(Hebrews 13:15)
though times sometime seem hard,
we can place all our trust in Him
His word will not return back void,
so in spite of our circumstances
remain faithful until the end,
His word is stronger than ever
and will never ever bend . . .

The Tates

Whenever it's time to worship GOD
satan seem ever present,
He sends His demon hesitate and vegetate
to distract us like a peasant,
He has a demon named imitate
whose main purpose is deceive us,
He has a demon name devastate
who is disruptive and come to grieve us,
His demon potentate comes to steal our focus
and His demon agitate comes to frustrate and to hold us . . .

What I Know Now

If I knew then what I know now
my life wouldn't be the same,
I'd be a far more better christian
way far ahead of the game,
I would be stronger than I've ever been
I would have avoided a lot of pain,
I wouldn't have been wet long behind my ears
life going quickly down the drain,
I would've long had access to heaven
GOD as my next of kin,
I would've run away from iniquity and transgression
and turned away from many sin,
if I knew then what I know now
I wouldn't have shed so many tears,
I would have drawn nigh unto the LORD
I would've long conquered all my fears,
I would've avoided some relationships
that weighed and held me down,
and stayed out of the sinking sand
but feet firmly planted on solid ground,
but what I know now I didn't know then
I'm on the right path growing,
I lean on JESUS for all my help
least now my blessings are flowing . . .

God Knows

Life is tinged with sadness
GOD knows for He placed us here,
but there will come a time one day
He will wipe away our tears . . .

Unspeakable Joy

I can walk black asphalt streets right now
but one day I'll walk on gold,
I'll see JESUS I'll have unspeakable joy
overwhelmed my eyes behold . . .

Magnificent Display

When I look at night and see the moon
beautifully GOD has made,
there is a burning feeling inside of me
no trial could ever fade,
how great thou are how great thou are
magnificent His display,
no words could e'er describe His glory
His stars glitter like birds at play . . .

The Savior

There is a name I call upon
His presence is always near,
I can carry to Him my every burden
for I know that He will hear . . .

Comfort

I know there is a better place
where problems don't exist
where peace do comfort all broken hearts
with a tender heavenly kiss . . .

Because You Live

Because you live
I can face tomorrow,
not worry about trials and trouble
nor grief which brings much sorrow,
not worry about physical or mental pain
which leave won't always last,
because you've promised a better day
I know this will also pass,
not worry about friends who let you down
for they are only flesh,
I'm meditating on you who brings me joy
and cause my mind to rest,
because you live
I have compassion for people who always seem ill,
no more property taxes
or collectors or bills,
no more trouble or trials
beer bottles or vials,
thank GOD I'm redeemed from all those life styles . . .

He Is The Way

In my weakness you're my strength
when I feel I can't go on,
when my situations hopeless
you're the one who makes me strong,
when so bound caught up in plight
darkness overwhelms my day,
JESUS makes it all alright
He is the light He is the way,
He's more than worthy of my praise
I live by faith there is no doubt,
when all my troubles leaves me dazed
my LORD and savior brings me out,
there's only one way to get to GOD
it's through my savior CHRIST,
who can wash with blood my awful sin
and change restore my life,
so if today seem dreary
and every step you take seem dark,
JESUS CHRIST He is the way give to Him your open heart . . .

More Than Able

GOD is no respecter of person
He loves me and He loves you,
His cup runneth over with mercy
He is more than able to bring us through,
in my daily walk with CHRIST
I've seen Him change so many lives,
when I couldn't walk myself
He picked me up when I got tired,
there's no help upon this earth
can change my life do what He's done,
I've searched wide and I've searched deep
and found no one below the son,
in His hands I place my care
because His judgment is always fair,
in the urgency of despair
GOD is good He's always there,
JESUS CHRIST He is the door
almighty GOD He is the hinge,
each day I knock continuously
that I might be let in,
that I might sneak a peak
at the mansions GOD has in store,
til then I'll just keep on trudging
praising Him for ever more,
GOD is no respecter of person
He loves me and He loves you,
His cup runneth over with mercy
He's more than able to bring you through . . .

Jehovah Jireh

Sometime it's easy to feel we are unworthy
to have GOD to walk by our side,
His cup runs over with mercy
I have no doubt He will provide,
out of all the dirt we've done
still He sent His only son,
to be the bridge between the gap
to save all if they would come,
many times people hear and read
it is no ordinary story,
but few there be that find that road
that leads up to His glory,
this book is just one witness
so some can't say they didn't know,
when they were content to live in darkness
for they did not want to grow,
JESUS nailed upon the cross
to break strongholds that keep you bound,
you cannot say you had no strength
to lift those weights which held you down,
for GOD gives us fresh fruit
to be special within His sight,
and though our faith be tried by fire
He will make it all alright,
so today we need be thankful
and praise JEHOVAH JIREH,
who gives of His abundance
He is awesome our provider . . .

True Friend

In heaven I am sure I will see you there
thanks for showing me you care,
a special friend until the end
one who forgives me of my sin,
some people claim to be an friend
but runs away from all your needs,
when they're around they smile and grin
their heart is selfish full of greed,
there is one who sticks closer than a brother
who is more than any friend I have,
He's there through any distress or trouble
and makes my heart feel glad . . .

My Deliverer

GOD you have always delivered me
you have never let me down,
even when I've turned my back on you
you've stayed close always around,
you have been better to me than I've been to myself
surely should have been dead and gone,
you have sustained me here I am today
had mercy when I was wrong,
even the wind and sea obey your voice
but yet you've given me a choice,
your spirit overwhelm me
and my eyes release it's moist,
weeping endureth for a night
but joy comes on tomorrow,
to relieve me of my stress and trouble
deliver me from all my sorrow . . .

Place Your Faith In God

Those waiting behind bars and steel
mans judgment isn't always just,
man will fail and let you down
who in the world then can you trust,
man looks into the future
past the right that you have done,
but quick to judge the wrong you do
to mark a victory won,
so place your faith in GOD
who will bring a new world order,
redo the structure of the earth
make streets clear like water,
what I sow I know I'll reap
took a while to grasp hold on,
each day is so important to me
for life is quickly gone,
we wrestle not against flesh and blood
the war is large and mean,
but the battle already has been won
through JESUS CHRIST our king,
man is weak and the heart is wicked
the word says who can know it,
in order to reap good within your spirit
you definitely has to sow it,
so place your trust in GOD
who will bring a new world order,
redo the heavens and the earth make streets as clear as water . . .

Stand Firm

When you don't feel like going
feels like all your strength is drained,
GOD will hold you up
and give you energy to sustain,
seems you're walking on sinking sand
and your emotions press you down,
GOD will pick you up
and place your feet on solid ground,
and when your problems become a nightmare
you don't know which way to turn,
and seems joy has forsaken you
tranquility a major concern,
when it appears you're in a storm
and winds are rigid stern,
that's the point GOD will manifest Himself
hold on and just stand firm.
(Heb 11:1) "Faith is the substance of things hoped for
and the evidence of things not seen."
We have a reason for this blessed hope
for our souls have been redeemed,
CHRIST died in hope we all might believe

cont - pg. 168

turn away from sin and come,
and follow Him though life be hard
look how far He's brought you from,
(Matthew 28:20) He said "lo I am with you always
even unto the end of the world."
So He will bring you through your trouble
worth more than a priceless pearl.
When it appears you're in a storm
and the wind is rigid and stern,
that is the point GOD manifests Himself
so hold on and just stand firm . . .

Words

As I search for precious words
that would make you want to wed,
words that are full of meaning
that no one has ever said,
words that are true
and place butterflies inside,
and as you read them touch your heart
and on your face there is a smile,
words that make you scream get excited jump for joy
words that will make you happy,
and any sadness will destroy
words that say I love you,
and you mean so much to me
words that will keep you in my life,
and make you stay don't want to leave
words that are deep and so very heart felt,
words that make you think of GOD
instead of me or yourself,
I wanted special words to ring noble and so true
words that make you think of GOD in everything you do . . .

Worth Waiting On

I look towards heaven and see white clouds
and sky magnificent blue,
a beautiful work made by GOD
the one who created me too,
love and joy and peace in the air
as one look up and He stare,
I am patiently waiting on JESUS to come
one day I'll move up there,
I will meet the twelve disciples
shake hands with Peter and Paul,
that's a day that is worth waiting on
I'll see my all in all . . .

Still Friends

I apologize for any inconvenience
in your life that I have caused,
I hope that we will stay friends
and no love between us lost,
if there's a way to repair the damage
to our friendship then I will,
just to take your pain and tears away
your best interest I hold it still,
we've had time to earn out differences
our friendship truly define,
a lot of times I was preoccupied
with many things going through my mind,
it's not that I didn't value our friendship
because I do and always will,
because you're special in my life
I care about you still,
GOD is my true leader
for I chose Him as my guide,
and I'd like to introduce you to Him
so let Him in your life,
He will never let you down
He'll do better than I can,
there is no loyalty such as His
that you'll find in any man,
lets still be friends mark it an adventure done
I'd like to introduce you to my father GOD,
AND JESUS CHRIST His Son . . .

Get A Grip

We need to get a grip on this busy world unkind,
look towards the hills from whence cometh our help
leave all our stress behind,
GOD uses rain sometime
to cleanse the world below,
if GOD ever turned His back on us
where oh where shall we go,
His cup runneth over with mercy
He has extended to us His grace,
some think tomorrow is promised
and do not seek the saviors face,
cars going back and forth
planes perturbing the air,
seem people has no love for one another
many do not even care,
but JESUS will come when most least expect it
so get your temple in order,
so upon accounting on judgment day
you want be there just to loiter . . .

Angel In The Midst

I'm here to exhibit the love of GOD
how can I be of help to you,
true friends are really hard to find
and faithful are a few,
you can call upon me anytime
even in the midst my rest,
the HOLY SPIRIT resides within me
I'll be there in your distress,
to help you conquer what you're going through
abiding by the word of the LORD,
to ease the struggles that overwhelm
though problems seem many and hard,
no weapon formed will prosper
GOD won't give you too much to bare,
I want to be an angel in the midst of your storm
because GOD loves you and He cares,
when life traps you in a situation
and it appears you're hopeless and stuck,
I'll be a friend in the midst of your trouble
don't hesitate to call me up . . .

Still Holding On

Today I am barely holding on
hoping GOD will strengthen my heart,
knowing all power lie within His hand
and truly how great thou are,
satan is attacking my faith
because I've been praying for something exact,
I've been constantly praying without ceasing
but it seems GOD has turned His back,
I know my time is not His time
He will answer whenever He feels,
but I know that He will answer soon
but my trouble has gotten me ill,
until then I'll keep holding on until my prayers avail
and when He answers still praise His name,
victory I'm sure to tell
the sun will shine into my life,
good days out weigh my bad
and when it does glorify His name,
rejoice in heart be glad
some days though in the valley,
GOD gives me strength I'm strong
doesn't matter what tricks satan throws against me,
I will still keep holding on . . .

I Can Always Go To Jesus

I can always go to JESUS
place my burdens in His hands,
my savior overcame this world
so I know He understands,
He attends to me with amazing grace
to make sure that I'm OK,
I've never called upon His name
and He just turned away,
I can always go to JESUS
and talk about anything,
He will wash all my dirt away
and leave me bright and clean,
He gives me freedom of choice
He even listens to me sing,
and He never jerks me around
like a puppet on a string,
I can always go to JESUS
He is my filling station,
He brings comfort, peace and joy to me
in any situation . . .

Through the Storms

After living this life a few of my years
after shedding victory tears,
through pain and suffering
worrying and fears,
I have learned to overcome
after being exalted,
then reduced to stubble
after surviving tremendous struggles,
holding on to wisdom with a heart as rubble
I have learned to overcome,
after being forsaken and left alone
putting fetters on my weaknesses to make me strong,
enduring humility when I was wrong
I have learned to overcome,
when faced with death
uncertain of life,
mind so weary from battling strife
problems in abundance,
finances tight
through CHRIST I have learned to overcome . . .

Every Knee Will Bow

He died upon a rugged stake
2 convicts by His side,
He rose again and lives today
which means Bruce Barton lied,
and many others who are in doubt
and lives without a GOD,
you play with fire
you will get burned,
and hell is mighty hot
there was one who was crucified,
and death grip had no hold
He died was buried and resurrected,
my GOD whom all will know
so put that in your pocket book,
and meditate on that
like lightening from the east to west
CHRIST is coming back . . .

Holy Love

When days are long and lonely
and no one seem to care,
GOD surrounds us with His love
for He is always there,
our sorrow far from burdening Him
draws out His tender love,
and comforts aching hearts down here
and draws us up above,
we walk by faith and not by sight
our aching heart He soothes,
He leads us through our troubled path
and all dark avenues,
He loves us so, I'm glad He cares
His heart can feel our grief,
He sends his love to comfort us and give our minds relief
and when our days seem dark and lonely
and no one seem to care,
GOD surrounds us with His holy love
a love beyond compare . . .

It Can Be Done

Doesn't matter how high the mountain is
with CHRIST it can be moved,
you can accomplish any task in mind
you set your heart to do,
It doesn't matter the distance you need to travel
with CHRIST you can achieve,
keep in vision whatever the desire is
have faith and just believe . . .

A Moment In Prayer

Each day may not turn out as you want it to,
there will be times that pressure
could easily cause an attitude,
so you must hold on during trying times,
remembering things eternal
leaving problems behind,
when the world seem cold
and no one seem to care,
what you need to do is take a moment in prayer.
People waste much time finding fault in others,
to no avail or prevail from experience they do discover
whoever said life would always be fair,
whatever happened to love thy brother
and His burdens help bare, when someone says something,
and your feelings has been hurt
whether we are at home, at work, or in church,
just forgive them by showing you care
and when given a chance take a moment in prayer . . .

Acknowledge God

(PROVERBS 3:11) "My son despise not the chastening
of the LORD;
neither be weary of His correction."
sometimes we need to be chastised to head in the right direction.
(PROVERBS 17:10) "A reproof entereth more into a wise man than
an hundred stripes into a fool."
Don't think to highly of yourself unlest you fall
acknowledge GOD in all that you do,
it is better to remain silent than be thought of as a fool
than to speak up and remove all doubt,
living is to obtain life and life to keep on living
and that's what it's all about.
Acknowledge GOD . . .

Thine Own Strength

LORD I'm weak and weary
sometime it's hard for me to stand,
and other times I know I'd fall
if you wasn't holding on to my hand,
and there are times that do approach
that my mind do fail to seize,
when the good that I ought do
seem way to much for me,
you know the weariness that fill
this ol' pain wrecked life of mine,
please be merciful to me O' LORD
and grant me strength from thine,
LORD you know the task ahead
I truly thank you for your love,
but grant me O 'GOD
for this one day
thine own strength from above . . .

A Heart Of Gold

LORD strengthen me
lead me in your ways,
keep me focused, rooted and grounded
so that I do not go astray,
place in me the mind of CHRIST
give me the will to sacrifice,
open my eyes so that I am aware
and I do not fall into satans snare,
give me the power to do your will
and be an example on how one should live,
manifest in me your spirit
give me charity so I can give,
and just help me walk upright
If it storm just let me stand,
let me be an advocate for love
and abide by all of your commands,
and forgive me if I sin
or I come up a little short,
but remind me to repent
from the bottom of my heart,
a good person I want to be
so let me have a heart of gold,
keep me humble very meek
and in the end reward my soul . . .

My Ever Present Help

I just want to be humble
and do that thing I know is right,
and to let GOD lead and guide me
through my problems and my plight,
I've tried life my way
and each time I've stumbled and fell,
each time I've had to look to JESUS
who reached down and gave me help,
without Him it would have been impossible
for me to stand today,
He walks with me and He talks with me
through life's most troubled way,
I've had to sit and be patient
one of the hardest things to do,
waiting on specific prayers to be answered
but knowing most certain He would bring me through,
today I am most humbled
and remain so very meek,
I constantly search within His word
just to hear Him speak . . .

He Wants Us To Be Faithful

God wants us to be faithful
He doesn't ask to much at all,
His yoke is really easy
and His burden is so small,
action speaks louder than bumper stickers
works is fuel to fill our faith,
and fear of the LORD should be so so great
don't be conservative when you pray,
through dreary days unfruitful years I shed so many tears
GOD has brought me through my trials,
and quieted down my fears
today I cling to Him He is all I have in hope,
He holds my hand through all my problem
and through my troubles helps me cope,
GOD just wants us to be patient
doesn't ask to much at all,
His yoke is pretty easy
and His burden is so small . . .

Due Praise

No other joy I know
than give to GOD His due praise,
He is worthy and He's fair
and He's patient towards my ways,
in this world He's been abused
than any other name,
yet He still dispenses mercy
in return for only pain,
what He expects from us is simple
though some reject His offer,
His name is used in vain and mocked
this land is full of scoffers,
soon so very soon
we are going to see the king,
if a boiler holds back pressure
it is bound to be full of steam,
the expression on many faces
in the end will be of shock,
to be rejected placed in hell
and the door eternal locked,
this poem is meant for you
be right in all your ways,
and strive to be the best you can
and give GOD His due praise,
life is just a vapor
very soon will disappear,
our destiny and our fate is close
oh yes! It's very near . . .

Alpha And Omega

He is my alpha and omega
my beginning and my end,
He is my grace and my mercy
He is a loyal faithful friend,
He is my anchor in the storm
He is my strength when I feel faint,
He is the one who hold my arm
when I think and feel I can't,
He is that calm, still, small voice
the one that teaches right from wrong,
He is the one that push me on
when I'm weak and don't feel strong,
you can search the earth and deep below
and you'll find no other greater,
than my beginning and my end
He is my alpha and omega . . .

Will There Ever Be

Will there ever be a place
in which a man can abide,
in which prejudice is ignorance
and just don't apply,
if GOD created us all equal
then who changed His rules,
who living stands up
and claims the ways of a fool,
we are all beautifully made
made in GOD'S image,
though some people's ways
will make a rattlesnake grimace,
will there ever be a day
a man can apply for a job,
and get it because of His experience
something color can't rob,
will there ever be a day
that all men surrender,
and show GODLY love one towards another

without referring to gender,
will there ever be a day
that creed isn't viewed,
but the contents of ones character
without Him being abused,
will there ever be a day
that all nations get along,
it will be in GOD'S kingdom
we'll sing the same patriotic song,
my dream is through life's journey
I can help someone else cope,
by freely sharing the gospel
introducing to them hope . . .

Be True

To win the race of life in CHRIST
ourselves we must apply,
and run hard with faith in all we do
until the day we die,
it doesn't matter how much wealth you have
don't gamble your soul and lose,
nor how many stocks and bonds you seem to have
you need to GOD be true,
all that CHRIST has done for us
how easily we forget,
satan deceives some with His gifts
and makes good hearts sin sick,
If you are on a ego trip
or whatever you are going through,
earthly things come to an end
you need to GOD be true . . .

Like A Sheep

As a sheep before the shearer is quiet
He opened not His mouth,
let your yes be yes and your no be no
leaving others minds in doubt,
sometime it's good to be quiet
and have innocence on your face,
and a melody within your heart
that glorify GOD with praise,
try to live a life that's straight
then your blessing will be great,
though you want to see GOD moving right now
you must be patient and wait,
like a sheep before the shearer is silent
be careful when you open your mouth,
it's not what goes in that stain the heart
but only that which comes out . . .

God Has Never

When life seem overbearing sometime
seem problems won't go away,
and the sun won't shine into your life
and cloud's seem always gray,
seem GOD won't listen to you pray
and hope is dwindling slim,
GOD has never turned His back on us
but we've turned our backs on Him,
in trouble we wonder why we hurt
and suffer from so much pain,
in good times we are happy with smiles
some live this life in vain,
we need to re evaluate our lives
when storms make life seem dim,
remember GOD has never
turned His back on us
but we've turned our backs on Him . . .

Miraculous Plan

GOD has a miraculous plan of escape
He has purposed just for you,
so the problem you are going through right now
GOD will bring you through,
and the only thing He ask of you
is go and sin no more,
and seek His face in spirit and truth
and your hope He will restore,
and all that satan has stolen from you
GOD says He'll give you more,
place you back upon the potters wheel
and remold you from the floor,
all you have to do right now
is repent and walk away,
from all those things which beset you
and wickedly makes you sway,
GOD has a miraculous plan of escape for you
but you have got to walk in faith,
don't worry about the problems you are going through now
because GOD will make away . . .

The Greatest Gift

My mother always told me be the best that I could be,
look towards GOD for all my answers
never hang in the street,
I am a witness of what GOD can do
for a life that was so torn,
He bandaged up my hurts and aches
and carried me through my storms,
today I am very grateful
I owe to GOD my very soul,
He brought me through the rugged streets
with no coat when it was cold,
He took the addiction of drugs from me
and restored me back to norm,
He took me through the valley of death
safely without any harm,
today I am rooted and grounded
now my storms doesn't blow me away,
that's because the greatest wisdom my mother ever gave me,
and that's of whom to pray . . .

The Greatest Of All Time

GOD talks to me early in the morn
through a precious little bird
who brings me a message so sweet,
to let me know I'm not forgotten
one day I will to fly free,
GOD rains on the poor and also rich
He loves us all the same,
I love to hear Him speak through thunder
reminds me of His fame,
He is the greatest of all time
there is nothing to compare,
everything that is dwell under Him
I love to breathe His air,
the stars scintillate sharply
in the midst of the night,
the sun is dark compared to Him
and all His marvelous light,
yet many are still vagrant
until GOD says avaunt,
and those who failed to call on Him
will suddenly be in want,
GOD is the tree of all life
I am a grape clinging to His vine,
and though I live I die to live again
for He is the greatest of all time . . .

God Wants Us To Grow

During difficult times we sometime become passive,
while waiting on a storm to pass,
and though it doesn't feel good when we are going through
the storm doesn't always last,
GOD knows life sometimes takes on sadness
there is no comparison to GOD'S parity,
no other with deep compassion
whose heart with such great charity,
He said He wouldn't leave nor forsake us
this we know by show,
He doesn't want us sitting idle minded
GOD wants us all to grow,
once we are saved it is not enough
there is plenty of work to do,
just don't sit back and relax in your church
and the furthest you make it is the pew,
take one day at a time with JESUS in mind
keep striving to make it over,
If we take one step GOD will take two
those are the ways of JEHOVAH,
He loves us dearly in His eyes we are precious
this we know by show,
He doesn't want us sitting idle minded
GOD wants us all to grow . . .

Finality

Our bodies as they get older
reveal life's fading stage,
unless JESUS extends His time toward us
seems we are in our final days,
this world may soon be over
and it offers no guarantee,
so don't stack wealth within this life
but take salvation which is free,
there is a younger generation
in for the shock of their life,
busy following trends impressing each other
instead of living and doing what is right,
man will become more wicked and more wiser
we are witnessing finality,
this world will soon be o'er
then we will live in eternity . . .

A New Creature

(2nd cor 5:17) "Therefore if any man be in CHRIST
He is a new creature:
old things are passed away;
behold all things are become new."
You no longer go to places you used to go today
you no longer say the things you used to say,
I will be glad to tell you
CHRIST never talked that way,
we are to put off our old behavior and exhibit a new change,
once we are saved and a baptized in JESUS
which is the name above all names,
if you sit idle you will fall down
the objective is to grow,
you need to find out all you can about CHRIST
be anchored and secure your soul . . .

A Friend

A friend is one you can lean on
when you have a problem and need a hand,
a friend will be there to make sure you don't fall
vice avers make sure that you stand,
a friend won't talk behind your back
or listen to someone who does a friend will be there
whatever you are going through,
just to provide you love,
a friend will share JESUS with you
because they know it's right,
a friend will make sure you press towards heaven
so you can enjoy eternal life,
a friend will won't entice you to do wrong
but instead encourage you to do right,
a friend will lift your spirit up
when you are feeling down,
a friend will help you no limit set
and mumble not a sound,
so check the company around you
see if they are eager to do dirt and sin,
if so they maybe an acquaintance of yours
but definitely not a friend . . .

Life Is Tinged

Life is tinged with troubles
this my savior know,
He gives us strength to stand up strong
against the storms that blow,
sometime we seem forgotten
though never are we forsaken,
be patient and wait on Him to move
His plan is in the making,
through your problems, pain and strife
let the son shine in your life,
by putting those things which beset you away
and striving to do what's right,
life is tinged with struggle
but we have help from up above,
who will cleanse us from all unrighteousness
and bathe us in His love . . .

His Abundant Grace

To be like JESUS is my goal
sometime I come up short,
I am only human—still
GOD expects me to do my part,
GOD'S grace is Him doing for me
what I don't deserve for Him to do,
His mercy is a little bit different
keep reading and I will explain it to you,
mercy is GOD not doing to me
what deserves to be done to me,
I thank CHRIST for His abundant grace
He died to set me free . . .

A Bitter End

Look around this world and see
the woe on peoples faces,
they try to cover it with pride
but the pain they just can't hide,
their heart is full of dread
seems they're like the walking dead,
there is a way that seemeth right unto a man
but the end there of is death,
it doesn't matter what status, prestige, color,
car you drive or wealth,
there is a road that leads to heaven
few there be that find it,
because their ways are not GOD'S ways
and their eyes satan has masterfully blinded,
misery is not prejudiced
and pain is not shy,
tears will not hold back
when the heart is ready to cry,
you can live now and totally die later
or live now and live again,
life is just a vapor
don't go speeding to a bitter end . . .

The Mentality Of A Thug

In this day and time
many are careless with their lives,
addicted to drugs, alcoholic, thugs
and temporary wives,
pill popping, club hopping, money fiends galore
full of pleasure, stacking treasure, and chasing every whore,
they portray themselves as hard
in their heart there is no love,
if you try to correct them they don't know JESUS
they have the mentality of a thug,
they are wired up and hyper
seem like they need a tranquilizer,
carry your sword where ever you go
and that's your equalizer,
they do most dirt at night
they are demons bound for hell,
it seem they always prosper
it seem they hardly ever fail,
good candidates for the grave
evil they always crave,
go down the street they are not hard to find
they love to rant and rave,
if you try to correct them beware
in their heart there is no love,
they refuse to meet our savior JESUS
for they have the mentality of a thug . . .

Too Much To Bare

LORD I am weary I've been strong and also brave,
I've been patient and long suffering
and my best I gladly gave,
I don't complain nor do I worry
nor do I say that it's unfair,
I keep pressing toward the mark of your calling
for I know you won't give me to much to bare,
I awake early in the morn
singing a praise within my heart,
and worshiping you with all sincerity
and oh what a wonderful start,
though the day seem long ahead
and I don't know the outcome,
I will glorify and lift you up
like David did in psalms,
often it seem my load is heavy
LORD help me not to fret,
nor get weary in well doing
use me as an angel LORD instead,
I can always turn to you
I know that you are always there,
I know that I am in your best interest

cont - pg. 205

and you won't give me to much to bare,
I am thankful you have not given me
exactly what I am due,
I would gladly give back a few of my years
for just one day of youth,
I won't complain I'll keep on pressing
I know your grace is fair,
thank you LORD for watching o'er me
and not giving too much to bare . . .

Sure Victory

Each day I adorn the armor of GOD
to fight the devil new,
sometime He deals my life a blow
so I back up then regroup,
but now I hold sure victory
we're fighting until the very end,
I place JESUS at the front of my battle
that way I'm guaranteed to win,
I love to black satan's eyes
stand back proud observe and smirk,
and watch GOD defeat my enemies
through His amazing work,
JESUS is coming soon
this is my epigraph,
the beginning of all wisdom
is to believe, live right
and fear the savior's wrath . . .

Roll Call

One day I'll close my eye's my friends
don't shed a tear of water,
I will have exited this troubled world down 'ere
and entered GOD'S holy portals,
I'll be standing near the pearly gates
when GOD do call the roll,
praying that you make it in
I'll be looking for your soul,
worshiping and rejoicing all day
praising GOD'S HOLY name,
thanking JESUS whom I LOVE
for the cross His blood did stain,
no more grief nor writhing storms
there will be no need for rain,
He will personally wipe away all tears
no more sorrow no more pain,
I'll be basking in His presence
inquiring about His fame,
the best feeling I will receive is in roll call
the day He calls my name . . .

Grief

The pain in mind produced by loss
misfortune with much sorrow,
a broken heart a loved one gone
it's hard to face tomorrow,
lamenting hard a void in life
no comfort this world can fill,
a reminder and a hard cold fact
that death is cruel and real,
death came suddenly and stole a life
their being was short and brief,
nothing can replace a loved one gone
not even a burial wreath,
I'll see that one again someday
when GOD calls for my soul,
and guide me to the splendor of heaven
and leave this flesh laying cold,
life is but a vapor
that only exist real brief,
and leaves a family so heart broken
no comfort there for grief . . .

One More Step

(1st Corinthians 15:58)
"Therefore my beloved brethren be ye steadfast,
unmovable always abounding in the work of the lord
for as much as ye know that your labor is not in vain."
(Galatians 6 :9) "And let us not be weary in well doing
for in due season we shall reap if we faint not."
Sometime you wonder if what you asked GOD for will ever come,
and sometime you feel like giving up
when the victory is almost won,
but there is an ample reward
for those who persevere,
therefore take just one more step
because your blessing maybe near,
sometime the struggle seem hard
difficult to keep going through pain and tears,
doubt truly test your faith
it's sometime hard to overcome your fear,
Isaiah 41:10 says "fear thou not; for I am with thee
be not dismayed."
you must be patient sometime and wait,
there is an ample reward
for those who persevere,
therefore take just one more step
because your blessing maybe near . . .

It's Just Me

I have to look in the mirror
sometime to see what's going on,
when things aren't going right in life
most often it's me that's wrong,
when I look at other people
tend to place on them the blame,
I need to look within my own self
and quit trying to go against the grain,
when I find fault in other people
if I would take time out and see,
that they are not the problem
majority of the time it is me,
when I awake early in the morning
and have a beam upon my shoulder,
I've got an ample amount of space
yet and still want others to move over,
when I'm having a rough day
and try to take it out on you,
and often criticize you
for any little thing you do,
I need to look straight into the mirror
to see what's going on,
whisper a little prayer to GOD
because most often it's me that's wrong . . .

God's Majestic Hand

(Isaiah 59:1) "Behold the LORD'S hand is not shortened
that it cannot save;
neither His ear heavy that it cannot hear."
He will turn ear to your supplication
if you are earnest and sincere,
often we need a moral inventory
to see if anything is hindering our prayer,
His word will not return void
and His judgment is always fair,
His cup runneth over with mercy
but we must reap whatever we sow,
His chastening is tough love to get our attention
so we can grow,
when GOD is moving
sometime we do not understand,
His ways are not our ways
sometime our plan is not His plan,
we as humans want things done immediately
GOD want jump at our every command,
we must be patient and wait sometime
and watch Him move with His majestic hand . . .

My Neighbor

I remember back in the good ol' days
if a person was in need,
a neighbor would take them food
and was more than eager to feed,
now times have changed
most neighbors aren't friendly any more,
they will deny you help grab their shotgun
and tell you to get away from their door,
it doesn't matter about my neighbors behavior
my love towards Him should be,
to do unto Him as I would myself
in hopes He would do the same for me,
today I pray for my neighbor
and harbor in my heart much love,
and let GOD direct our paths
with His kindness from up above . . .

No Regret

Sometime you must push harder
to reach the mark ahead,
though it feels sometime you are at your limit
and want to give up instead,
there is nothing worth having that's easy
contrary it's hard to get,
but once you have achieved your goal
you can enjoy it with no regret,
in life there are no boundaries
or no limit in which you can soar,
once you've tasted sweet success
you will work harder to get even more,
if you would take time out to pray
GOD truly will bless your soul,
He will give out of His abundance
that you would not have room to hold,
there is no limit to what GOD can do
if you put Him foremost in your life,
He will order your steps bless you with health
so stay focused and keep doing what's right
sometime you must push harder
to reach the mark ahead,
though it may feel you are at your limit
you'll enjoy it with no regret . . .

Faith Of A Mustard Seed

Knowing when we die
is to be present with CHRIST,
gives us much energy
to do right in this life,
when an area of short coming arise
and like a tornado twirl,
I've got way more faith than a mustard seed
cause CHRIST overcame this world,
I'm holding on and won't let go
for He is all I've got,
His holy word I store in my heart
for any stumbling block,
when an area of short coming arise
and like a tornado twirl,
I've got far more faith than a mustard seed
cause CHRIST over came this world . . .

Soar

The devil is busy in this world
to entertain our minds,
to keep us distracted from GOD
by wasting majority of our time,
thus giving Him the ultimate chance
to try to steal our soul,
to keep love out of our hearts
and keep us bitter cold,
If JESUS isn't on your mind
that makes you eligible to sin,
out of the abundance of the heart the mouth speaketh
so cursing comes from within,
so we must put on the whole armor of GOD
to fight the battles of life,
and to step over the stumbling blocks that satan sets
and soar to unlimited heights . . .

Yes He Will

As you are about your business today
take a little time to pray,
and watch the mountains move over
for GOD will clear the way,
glorify His name
in your heart sing a hymn of praise,
place your problems within His hand
and GOD will clear the way,
you have come through many obstacles
in Him you've placed your faith,
and you know beyond a shadow of doubt
that GOD will clear the way,
He won't leave you nor forsake
give Him your baggage and your freight,
place all your trust and faith in Him
and know that GOD will clear the way,
yes He will . . .

Well Done

(psalm 84:11) No good thing will He with hold
for them who walk upright.
Each day I go from strength to strength
each night from might to might,
satan tries to attack often
it's His nature for Him to fight,
but the battle is not mine, it is the LORD'S
so everything will be alright,
when this life is o'er
and I depart from this ol' shell,
I hope JESUS pats me on the back
and reward me with His greatest gift that is eternal life,
and invite me into His chamber
to reside within His light . . .

The Gift Of God

By grace are you saved through faith
not work lest any man should boast,
it is the gift of GOD for all mankind
for our creation He loves the most,
His word should change our lives each day
bring hope to troubled souls,
if we adhere to whatsoever He says
your heart should not wax cold,
He sent His only begotten son
to wash away our sin,
and destroy the fetters that satan hold
conquer death and win,
salvation is the gift of GOD
for trouble will not end,
once He sanctifies keep your hand to the plow
and never turn back again . . .

How Do You Feel

When you see people suffering
and their life is a troubled train,
seems when it rains it pours
can you even feel their pain,
when someone has a testimony
about a sickness that's in their life,
right now they are going through something
can you feel their strife?
When someone is homeless and hungry
and asking for a few of your coins,
do you turn them away?
Can you even feel their storm?
When someone is displaced
because fire engulfed their home,
do you feel their struggle
knowing they are facing it all alone?
Life sometime give hardship
that we feel we don't deserve,
when it appears life is going straight
life can suddenly take a curve,
the problems I aforementioned
are present and also real,
when it is raining in someone else life
tell me how do you really feel?

Freely

Freely give your hearts devotion
to the one it's worthy of,
JESUS CHRIST our LORD AND SAVIOR
who freely gives us love,
He died and rose to bring redemption
to save a wretch like me,
He is the ultimate my sacrifice
in whom I am set free,
my soul rejoices for all He's done
laid His life down for all men,
holds the keys to death and the grave
I'm no longer bound by sin . . .

Peace At Last

Through your grace I pray I grow
like JESUS CHRIST I want to be,
within my heart my spirit flows
it feels so good like summers breeze,
I'm holding firm to CHRIST in faith
no greater love reigns o'er all,
He is supreme He is so great
He tends each day our every call,
my hope is built on JESUS name
He died and rose to set me free,
this world yet since to be the same
till through the clouds He comes for me,
one day together we'll give Him praise
bow down and worship before His throne,
and learn the mystery of His ways
peace at last be finally home . . .

Be Compassionate

you need to be compassionate
instead of fault finding and vindictive,
because nonconstructive criticism
could render you restrictive,
we need to be careful
of what we say of each other,
we need to encourage instead of discouraging one another,
we are all created in the image of GOD
although some do not act like CHRIST,
so their obedience is very limited
till their actions are cruel to life,
but in spite of what they do
keep the focus on your self,
and build a fortune here on earth
that leads to eternal wealth,
some are very eager to war
but never eager to peace,
but I wish worldwide all wars be over
and disagreements cease,
be compassionate the war is not against man's flesh
but against the enemy,
He's the author of trouble and confusion
the one who hates one's life at peace . . .

Life Will Give

Do you know your purpose in life
can you put your finger on it,
are you feeling in despair
are you feeling down and lonely,
here is a word of advice
that I hope will be your help,
there is nothing under the sun that's new
the battles within yourself,
you can achieve anything you want to do
your season is here so move,
GOD is about to give increase
tell satan to turn it loose,
there is going to be much overflow
to spill on those nearby,
and joy will over flood your heart
so much it will make you cry,
put all your trust in JESUS
He alone will bring you through,
put Him first and fore most in your life
and in everything you do,
so just keep on pressing
sometime it will seem you've failed,
go on inspire of your circumstances
life will give, then all is well . . .

Joy Will Never End

The love we've experienced here on earth
is nothing compared to then,
we all will have a glorious body
and perfect in GOD'S sight again,
worshiping, rejoicing never to die my friend
no more turmoil no more trouble, trials or no more danger,
we all will have pure peace in mind
we all will be as angels,
inquiring within His temple
curiosity of His mysteries,
asking questions of unknown answers
that have happened in past history,
the love we've known while here on earth
is nothing compared to then,
we all will have a glorious body
where joy will never end . . .

I've Learned To Be Content

I have seen people come and go
GOD'S grace is still the same,
doesn't matter what you are going through
sufficient through joy and pain,
sufficient in trouble, sufficient in sickness
sufficient in peace and health,
sufficient in ups sufficient in downs
sufficient in life and death,
we've lived good lives time is short yes it is almost spent,
I have been abased I've been abound
but I have learned to be content,
I've seen despair and had no hope
and wished that life would cease,
I've had cars, I've had money, and also drugs
and still I had no peace,
I've been locked up for what was due
and had no one to help,
I've waged war against the world alone
and the enemy I had was self,
I've been hungry had no clothes
had no meat nor even rolls,
then one day CHRIST entered my heart
and gave my life a brand new start,
took away my frown and left a grin
His grace is sufficient now in all things,
I have learned to be content . . .

Fire Baptized

Today there is gifts that I do bare
cause I took upon His yoke,
and I am saved I'm sanctified
and filled with the HOLY GHOST,
there is work that I need do
I need to love like JESUS CHRIST,
I need to help someone along the way
and help to change their life,
if someone is hurt and crying
then I hope to make them laugh,
I want to be a light so bright
on someone's darkened path,
It's only by the grace of GOD
that I'm here and I'm alive,
He picked me up and turned me around
and now I'm FIRE BAPTIZED . . .
God desire true holiness and faithfulness from you,
He deserves all your praise and worship
In everything you do.
He deserves a pure and Holy Life
That has been set apart,
He deserves your unconditional love
From the bottom of your heart,
I hope to hear Him say well done
You are worthy of the prize
Because you turned your life around
and now you're FIRE BAPTIZED . . .

I WOULD LIKE TO GIVE HONOR AND GLORY TO MY LORD AND SAVIOR JESUS CHRIST FOR THE GREAT THINGS HE HAS DONE. I WOULD LIKE TO THANK ALL OF YOU WHO BELIEVED IN ME OVER THE YEARS, AND I PRAY THIS TALENT GOD HAS GIVEN ME BLESSES SOMEBODY'S MIND, HEART AND SOUL.